A DISCUSSION ON BASIC JEWISH PROBLEMS

A
Challenge
to
Jewry

by

Joseph L. Tepper

VANTAGE PRESS, INC., NEW YORK

TO ALBERT EINSTEIN

One of the Greatest of All Time

CONTENTS

INTRODUCTION

The great French Revolution with its aftermath, the uprisings
in the middle of the nineteenth century, generated and stored up
the forces that brought the Haskala to Eastern Jewry and crashed
the gates of ignorance and superstition which isolated them from
the West. The Nazi revolution near the middle of the twentieth
century with its incalculable evil to the rest of the world, un-
hinging civilization, not merely exterminated half of European
Jewry but stunned the intellectual equilibrium of the rest of the
Jews the world over. The first effect was to reverse the march
toward progress and enlightenment which was set in motion by
the Haskala movement of the nineteenth century which pro-
ceeded apace until the Nazi holocaust.

Like the shock and grind of a violent application of pressure
on a mechanical break, this international nightmare bewildered
and constricted Jewish mentality. It threw it into its current chaos
and confusion. The secular way of life vouchsafed by the emancipation from mental serfdom in the course of almost a century,
the natural aptitude toward progress and enlightenment, the Jew
is now told, is sinful and a menace to his spiritual redemption.
He is belabored to return to ghetto fundamentalism and fit himself into a parochial garb and mask. He is thus threatened with a
split personality—the secular twentieth-century way of life he is
now accustomed to, on the one hand, and on the other, his affirmation of and identification with the Orthodox Code of the 613
(Taryag) ordinances and prescriptions which are multifarious and
well-nigh impossible to live up to. These in fact he had mostly
ignored. If he is a person of character and conscience, it is bound
to create a guilt complex that brings with it a form of schizo-
phrenia and ambivalence.

v

To expose and check the folly of this trend is the object of this book. The method is dialectical; a discussion and analysis of the tripod on which rest the three fundamental and vital problems confronting Jews everywhere: anti-Semitism, the advent of Medinas Israel, and the state of the Jewish religion. The principal endeavor is to bring these problems into a proper focus in relation to everyday living in this present era and thus bring about a synthesis and harmony in our thinking and actions.

The author is painfully aware that the task is bigger than himself. But he hopes that by sparking the discussion it will interest others who may be able to bring greater ability and more scholarship and brilliance to the task. The reward this writer hopes for is to bring the subject to the fore and set in motion its further consideration and discussion.

Finally, he wishes to give emphatic assurances that while opinions set forth herein are as unequivocal and as clear and sharp as he knew how to phrase them, there is no intention to offend or affront any individual or group as such. He has not the slightest desire to get involved in polemics nor to seek notoriety. He may err about some or many things he says, but there is no other reason for saying them than deep conviction and sincerity.

J.L.T.

PREFACE

I PROPOSE TO SHOW:

1. That anti-Semitism is inherent in our present economic-political system. It will inevitably be circumvented by the coming changes in the evolution of that system.

2. That while we should aid the new state of Israel to the utmost of our power, our relations to it should be refocused in the perspective of Jewish life in the Diaspora.

3. That our religion is antiquated and not in keeping with the spirit of our time.

PART ONE

CHAPTER I

STEREOTYPES

1

Anti-Semitism goes back to the earliest period in history, but its pattern and design has hardly undergone any change. This is the disheartening and ominous aspect of the problem.

The phenomenon takes on four stages. Each of these stages dovetails into the other. First, political or economic pressure, or both, compel an already established Jewish community to pull up stakes and migrate to another more promising and congenial environment. The second is the orientation or adjustment to the new environment—a period of struggle, self-denial, and taking root. The third is the harvest— success, fulfillment, self-assertion, and entrenchment. The fourth and final stage is when troubles start and end in persecution, discrimination, and, in some instances of the past, with expulsion. The intervals between these dire stages may be decades or centuries. Whether the liberation from Egypt is fact or myth, the writer of the episode followed this same tragic cycle to its end. First was the famine that drove Jacob with his family to Egypt, and then the struggle for orientation and adjustment, after which they prospered and became important, and finally the enslavement and persecution. The same doleful story is repeated in the Spanish period of Jewish history, although there the golden age of glory lasted several centuries. Perhaps that was due to the absence of what is called Christian civilization and humanitarianism! The same melancholy parallel repeats itself later in England, France, the German states, and other parts of Europe. Can we ever escape this accursed cycle?

There is still another parallel. Analyze the complaints and charges of our enemies. We are a gregarious people, clannish, and not able to fuse with others; or we are pushers, aggressive, intruders in other people's affairs, too loud, gesticulating, and, on the whole, a bad influence. If we came from the East, we are poor, filthy, ignorant, and medieval. If we come from the Western part of Europe, we are too affluent, ostentatious, and parasitical. We spawn capitalism and all its evils of exploitation and oppression, and we are at the same time authors of all unrest and subversive movements, such as anarchism, socialism, communism. In other words, as radicals, we conspire to destroy ourselves as capitalists! In this fashion, our enemies have pinned on us the most bizarre and contradictory charges. Take the often repeated lamentation of the anti-Semites: The repressed handful of persecuted, abused Jews are a menace to the stalwart, incorruptible, and invincible Aryans. William Marr, of Hamburg, started this canard in 1873, in a pamphlet titled *The Victory of Judaism over Germanism.* The theme caught on. Hilaire Belloc sanctioned this thesis by saying: "The Jews are obtaining control, and we will not be controlled by them." In summary, the charges against the Jews by the so-called intellectual anti-Semites, Hilaire Belloc, Madison Grant, G. K. Chesterton, Houston Stewart Chamberlain, Lothrop Stoddard, and others, are that (a) Jews are a disintegrating force in the political, moral, and cultural life of the countries in which they reside; (b) they seek to dominate and monopolize everything for their own enrichment; (c) they conspire to destroy Christianity.

On the other hand, they claim that their kind, the Aryans, are the superior race in every detail, that the intermixture with Jews has a demoralizing effect, and that the Semitic strain in art, culture, literature, and manners and morality is deleterious.

Again, the paradox: the Jew is superior and "gets the best of us," or he is inferior and decadent and "drags us down." The gripes of the American brand of anti-Semite, especially the professional ones like the Coughlins, Edmondsons, the Pelleys, Winrods, and Gerald L. K. Smiths, use variations of the same theme.

There is something invidious, sinister, and mysterious about the subject of anti-Semitism. From time to time, other minorities have been persecuted or discriminated against and disliked, but not with such consistency or intensity as the Jews. In all periods of recorded history this issue has been on the agenda of public discussion. Even those who had no contact with Jews and had not known any, hated them on hearsay. From time to time in the present era, various public agencies have conducted polls on the subject, and invariably the findings are most discouraging. Two such polls conducted by *Fortune* magazine, in 1947, show that an alarming percentage of the population in the United States feels that the Jews have too much economic and political power, implying that they should be curbed. This prevails among the rank and file, but you might have expected something better at the higher levels, especially from those who mold public opinion, the literati. Surely, they should be above vulgar and degrading race prejudice; yet they are as vulnerable to this social blight as the common herd. Consider, for instance, the sneers and poisonous darts of Henry Adams; the shameless outbursts of Theodore Dreiser in the middle thirties; the contemptible Jewish types in some of the stories by Willa Cather and Edith Wharton; and, above all, the bitterness shown by Thomas Wolfe, whose life is supposed to have been greatly influenced by a Jewess. These are only a few among many other novelists, journalists, and publicists in this country and other countries.

The outstanding and acknowledged characteristics of the Jew from time immemorial are his crusading genius for justice and his sympathy with the underdog. In every political, economic or social conflict between a suppressed minority and organized power, whether church, royalty or capitalism, the Jew invariably is on the side of the victim, unmindful of the risk to himself. To cite just a few illustrations: at the start of the industrial era, a bitter conflict arose between the landed aristocracy, who then held the scepter of power, and the rising industrial classes, the bourgeoisie. The Jews wholeheartedly threw themselves into the struggle against the landed gentry. Later, however, when the bourgeoisie triumphed, they turned against the Jews because they gave them too much competition.

In the struggle for freedom against the Czars in Russia, the Jews were the most fearless and self-sacrificing; indeed, that was the main pretense for the government's persecution of them. That, however, did not stop the Russian peasantry from ganging up from time to time to make pogroms. The father of scientific socialism, Karl Marx, and its early most brilliant interpreters and exponents, were mostly Jews. Yet, when it became better understood and more popular among the masses in Europe, there sprang up so-called Christian-Socialist units, with the avowed purpose of curbing the Jewish influence. Then, too, let us ask: How much real concern and distress did the powerful socialist and liberal movements display over the plight of the Jewish masses in the hour of their greatest peril in Europe during and immediately following World War II? Consider the strange in-

[5]

difference to the pleas of a couple of hundred thousand Jews in the D.P. camps to be allowed to emigrate to some of the vast territory under the control of those many groups. It is hard to suppress a feeling of bitterness over the awareness that there is a strong, impenetrable, monolithic dislike of the Jew everywhere.

What, in the main, is behind this venomous hatred of a whole people? Later, I shall have some comments on the mass hatred engendered by the scapegoat function of the Jew in the Middle Ages and in modern times. That will account for the unpopularity and dislike of the Jew by the third estate, the lower industrial classes, and the peasantry. In the case of some of the most notorious and vicious anti-Semites, personal explanations are advanced. For instance, Bagdan Chmielnicki, leader of the Cossacks during their rebellion against the Poles in 1648, was responsible for the slaughter of a quarter of a million Jews. He is alleged to have been mistreated by some individual Jew, and he later took it out against all of them. Similarly, Hitler is also supposed to have been offended by some Jews in his days of want and poverty. Whether these tales are true or not, it is likely that some Jew-haters have avenged themselves bitterly against all Jews for some real or fancied grievance against some of them. Other anti-Semites are of the crackpot variety, cultists out to save Christianity from the Devil, while with a great many others it is a profession or business. It often pays well. Then, there are what may be termed opportunist anti-Semites. They, themselves, may be free from anti-Semitic bias, but they pursue it or even promote it as a matter of policy. A classical case in point is that of Bismarck. He was carrying on a political feud with the Catholic party—the Centrists—over control of education in Germany, a traditional issue with Catholics. It was then, and is now, a cardinal principle of the church to educate the youth. Bismarck stood for state control of education. He also had differences with the Liberal Party under the leadership of Lasker, a Jew, who failed to back him up in his controversy with the Catholics, which he felt he was losing. Out of peeve and resentment, and, also, as a diversion and to save face, he came out in support of anti-Semitism. There are numerous other instances like it in other countries, although not as conspicuous. Even in the United States, during the height of Ku Klux Klan political activity, some politicians openly advocated discriminatory laws against Jews and otherwise followed the anti-Semitic line. Some do it now, when

[6]

they feel that through prejudice against Jews they may gain votes.

2

This is a very brief and perhaps inadequate sketch of several types of anti-Semites and the reasons and circumstances that motivate them. Having a clue to these motives makes it possible sometimes to circumvent them. But there is a type of hatred, a deep, galvanized, mass-dislike, that is as puzzling as it is ominous. Because it is mystifying, it defies proper definition and analysis. It can only be described by its reactions in given circumstances. Take the case of Germany. It is simply incredible that the Christian nations could have stood by and witnessed the slaughter and extermination of a whole people in the Hitler period. Conceding the fact that the smaller countries were too terrified to make any move, what about the big powers? Of course, we must thank our stars that the Jews were not the primary cause for starting World War II. But it is a tragic and melancholy fact that a whole people was being torn to shreds within sight of a so-called civilized world, and no one as much as tried to stay the claws of the beast. Yet that isn't really the worst of it. What followed is even more callous because it is deliberate and calculated and portends greater indifference and cruelty, if not sadism. It is what happened after the nightmare was over and the magnitude of the horror—the slaughter in cold blood of over five million innocent and harmless men, women, and children—became known. The usual reaction of human beings, following disaster, is to do all in their power to comfort, protect, and shelter the survivors, particularly those suffering from shock, without inquiring into their race or religion.

The end of World War II found several hundred thousand shocked and demoralized Jewish victims. For over three years after the war these victims were kept in military camps and referred to as "displaced persons." There was not enough charity and humanity in the entire group of great and civilized nations to open their gates to them and give them asylum. What excuses were given for this hardness of heart? Here is an example. It is typical, except that it is more candid and more blunt than others. In Pretoria, South Africa, Jan Christiaan Smuts told Parliament on April 24, 1947, that he deeply sympathized with Jewish suffering and pledged to do his best toward the creation of a Jewish national home in Palestine. "The fate of the Jews," he said, "was the greatest tragedy of our age." He felt it was possible to arrive at some solution by which the Arab and the Jew could live together in Palestine. However, he was not so sure about Jews and South Africans. He opposed Jewish immigration into South Africa, he said, because it would "overload" the country with Jews and create anti-Semitism (*Commentary*, May, '47, page 471).

A special supplement of *The Nation* (May 17, 1947, 589) on "The Palestine Problem," under the sub-title: "Are There Other Countries to Which the Jew can Migrate?" lists: Argentine, area 1,085,000 square miles, population over 14 million; Brazil, area 3,276,000 square miles, population over 45 million; Mexico, area 764,000 square miles, population over 25 million; Chile, area 297,000 square miles, population over 5 million. To these we can add Australia, area nearly 3 million square miles, population over 7 million; Canada, area 3,694,863 square miles, population nearly 12 million. Yet, there was no room for a few hundred thousand harried and tortured Jews! The point is not whether Premier Smuts of South Africa, one of the most enlightened and humanitarian statesmen, was an anti-Semite, or whether he was really afraid that a few hundred thousand Jews would "overload" his country, as he expressed it. If it had been up to him, there would have been no question of opening the doors, at least, to some of the displaced persons. Actually, he feared public opinion and did not want to risk the fate of his government. This is neither a guess nor a state secret. In 1939, General J. B. M. Hertzog joined hands with the notorious anti-Semite Dr. F. Daniel Malan and his National Party on a platform that combined racialism and anti-war propaganda and gave Smuts a very hard fight. Since then Smuts' government was defeated, and Malan's put into power.

The same situation prevailed in many, if not most, of the other countries. It is not a deep, dark secret that if the late administration in Washington had had its way, it, too, might have made it possible for many displaced persons and refugees to enter the United States. But it dared not antagonize public opinion. It was even wary and timid in the way it asked Congress to open the gates ever so little to enable a few additional refugees to enter through the Stratton Bill. They knew, too, how readily the opposition party could pounce on them if they came out boldly in favor of a more liberalized immigration policy. In fact, the 80th Congress administered a slap in the face to Jewry by adopting amendments to the Bill—amendments that limit the number of Jewish refugees to be admitted, to only 6,000.

3

If this picture is not overdrawn, and if public opinion is as bitter as that against the Jew, it gives rise to these terrifying inquiries: How secure are the Jews here? How strong are our ramparts? On the face of it, there are many reassuring answers. This country has strong traditions of freedom and fair play, and an all-embracing Constitution and Bill of Rights. Has this given adequate protection to the Negroes in their civil rights? Has it prevented lynchings? Did it secure to Frank in Georgia a fair trial or save him from being lynched? Did it prevent the Ku Klux Klan from running amuck about two decades ago?

Another is that the Jews have a good press. That is a comfort. But let us not forget that the reason for this is not so much for love of us, but because we are a very important factor in retail business, which furnishes so much of the advertising. If it were not for this, many of the newspapers would handle us differently. Just imagine, if you can, what the Hearst, McCormick, the Patterson, and some other papers would be saying about the Jews. Even now, when advertising is a great check on these papers, they spill over at times, as in the O'Donnell episode in the *New York News.* Yet the protection and immunity the Jewish population enjoys from the press is a great source of strength, except in times of stress and tension due to economic dislocations. At such times, even the big monopolies and corporations, who really run things, get nervous and fearful that their economic grip on the nation will be protested by the public. At such times they are old hands at encouraging and creating subversive movements to divert attention from themselves to some scapegoats. Witch-hunts, anti-foreign drives, Red-baiting, and race riots are examples. As scapegoat material Jews have been made use of over and over again.

Today, Jews do have a great many avowed friends. The late Charles Edward Russell, the late President Franklin Delano Roosevelt, Eleanor Roosevelt, James G. MacDonald, Earl G. Harrison, and Bartley C. Crum can be numbered among the sincere friends, as well as many other enlightened statesmen, radio

[9]

commentators, editors, publicists, scientists and philosophers. This total sounds impressive, but actually it is a drop in the bucket. Most of the other friends and defenders of the Jew are political friends who are influenced by the Jewish vote, especially in communities where it can swing a balance. However, the total Jewish population is only about four per cent of the population of the United States, and concentrated in a few areas. Besides, the political friendship is notoriously unreliable. It is a friendship of convenience, and fades out when it stops paying dividends. There are also a number of so-called defense organizations, such as the Conference of Christians and Jews, the Anti-Defamation League, and various other anti-racial movements calculated to offset and expose anti-Semitism and Fascism. Some of these are subsidized by Jews who do not intend again to be caught napping as they were in Germany. But that is not any better than having to build a wall around oneself to prevent beasts from breaking in, or having to sleep with a gun at one's side. It is better than no defense at all, but it is indeed a restless slumber.

The curious thing about this impenetrable mass dislike of the Jew is that in hundreds of thousands of cases individual Jews make desirable and happy adjustments with their non-Jewish neighbors and friends. From this springs the often quoted satirical phrase: "Some of my best friends . . ." and the saying that when there are ten Jews in a community, one of them is picked for mayor, but when there are a thousand, they are considered objectionable. This writer, like many thousands of others in Jewry, established some of the most beautiful and life-long friendships with non-Jews; yet, in our relationship to the community as a whole, we are always made to feel in one subtle way or another that we are outside the charmed circle. It is common knowledge, and has been proven time and again, that many people, and even entire groups, who have never known Jews and never dealt with them, are still antagonistic to them. When asked for the reason, they are unable to account for it. In other words, Jews are presumed to be bad until they prove themselves good.

CHAPTER II

EXPLANATIONS FOR ANTI-SEMITISM

Isn't it time that the Jews made a sincere and objective effort to answer this conundrum? Is it sufficient for them to blame the Gentile for everything and absolve themselves from all blame? This isn't just happening in our time. It has been the order of events for several thousand years in different parts of the world. As has been shown, each cycle of anti-Semitism has a monotonous and tragic resemblance to the one that preceded it. Few subjects have been written about and discussed more than anti-Semitism. One can easily assemble a whole library of books and pamphlets on the subject. Unfortunately, little of this literature is in a temperate or objective vein. It is either malicious attack, based on vicious mendacity, or equally fulsome eulogy. Obviously, neither approach is conducive to a sound and constructive consideration of the subject. Indeed, it is very difficult for any Jew to consider this matter in a clear, impartial state of mind. His cupful of misery has run over too often to expect it of him.

Yet this writer will attempt a dispassionate analysis of the basic causes of anti-Semitism—even at the risk of being misunderstood and taking the chance of being charged with anti-Jewish bias by some neurotic superpatriots.

First, I want to dispel an ancient, traditional misconception on the subject. That is the Jesus crucifixion theory. Naturally, the constant reiteration of the crucifixion story in Sunday schools and by enemies of the Jews and the defensive arguments of rabbis does not help. It is sheer nonsense to argue that this single episode that is supposed to have happened over nineteen hundred years ago—if it happened at all—is behind this persistent and increasing hostility. The fires of race hatred demand a constant supply of fuel to keep them burning. Past memories may aggravate them, but not keep them going. There seem to be no hate movements kept alive today either against the Italian people, or against the Vatican for the beastly acts of the Borgias, whose evil deeds are historical facts and much nearer to our day. Nor is there race hatred of Catholics for the massacre on St. Bartholomew's Eve. Nor is there a hate movement against the Spanish people, or the Catholic Church, because of the terrible Inquisitions. These are historical facts and not as tenuous as the alleged crucifixion of Jesus. One may call a Jew a "Christ killer" but that is on a par with insulting a cripple on the score of his affliction. It is hardly ever the primary cause of the quarrel. That explanation is an over-simplification without historical authenticity. There is no analogous instance wherein a whole people is held up to obliquity and scorn for something that its ancestors did, or are presumed to have done, in the past.

The true cause lies elsewhere. Cruel fate placed the Jews at the crossroads of conflicting commercial currents, and in such a position they became the target for attack and abuse. In the earliest stages of history they became the world's most skilled traders—too expert for their own good. Their race brothers, the Phoenicians, built the ancient cities of Tyre and Sidon and became formidable in trade, their ships plying to ancient Greece, Italy, and Spain. Wherever they went, they built trading posts, some of which became great cities. Cadiz and Marseilles had their start as such posts. Our modern alphabet came from them. In like manner, they were hated and derided by their contemporaries.

In modern times, too, the Jew contributed mightily to the building of the great commercial empires of the world, the brilliant and powerful world capitals, namely: London, Paris, Berlin and Vienna. Jewish contribution to American industry and commerce, to the building up of the great American cities—New York, Chicago, Philadelphia—is proverbial. Wherever the Jew goes, he quickens the pace of growth and progress. Here is a graphic and visual example. Palm Beach has been a thriving winter resort in Florida for over a century. Jews were looked upon askance, and their coming was not encouraged. Then the Miamis, about seventy miles south, were opened up less than fifty years ago, and, while not ostensibly encouraged, nothing was done to keep Jews out. Due almost entirely to Jewish enterprise, Miami Beach is today one of the outstanding winter resorts in the world. It is an architectural marvel and is fast developing into a cultural center. Its combined population with Miami is about ten times that of the much older, but more aristocratic, Palm Beach area. Some will say that this has not been an aesthetic gain. But is

[12]

progress measured by the fine and beautiful things that only the few may enjoy, or the more ample facilities made available to the masses?

Yet, with all that, the Jews, like the ancient Phoenicians, are hated and derided. Why? It is largely because, as peerless retail merchants, as the conveyor belt between the large producer and the consumer, the Jew is the first to catch the missiles of criticism and resentment for high prices and poor quality, although in a larger sense he has no control over any of these factors.

The scapegoat position of shock absorber between the real masters and exploiters and their exploited victims was foisted upon the Jews back in the Middle Ages. In those days, when all economic secular power was concentrated in the hands of the church and the robber feudal barons, the Jew was denied nearly all of the legitimate channels of earning a livelihood. He could not own land, and the doors of the craft guilds were closed to him. He was pushed into a groove, where he was forced to do all the dirty and unpleasant tasks for both the feudal lord and the church. The church sanctimoniously forbade the lending of money or charging of interest. It suited the church to have the Jew perform those functions. Similarly, the lord of the manor, the duke, and the prince, employed the Jew to do the sweating and exploiting of the peasantry. All week the Jew discharged his financial duties among the peasants, the princes, the big land-owners, and the church. On Sunday, the church held him up to contempt as a heretic and a leech. Some of the kings and over-lords played the diabolical goose-fattening game. They let the Jews fatten, and then extorted their gains from them by torture or deliberate expropriation. The technique is ably described by Sir Walter Scott in *Ivanhoe* (the way in which Rebecca's father Isaac was tortured), and in many other books that describe the life of that period. In many instances, entire Jewish cities were forced to pay large tribute, on one pretense or another. In other instances, they were robbed and expelled from the country.

On the other hand, I do not mean to convey the impression that the Jewish role was, as a tool for the overlord, altogether an unwilling one. Destiny had long prepared the Jew for it. His apprenticeship in the arts of trading had begun centuries back. At no time was trading noted for its ethics. The two are allergic to each other. Even in this advanced age, when business methods are standardized and more refined, it's "dog eat dog." When the victor happens to be a Jew and the victim a non-Jew, the latter yowls and hurls anti-Jewish charges. During the Middle Ages, also known as the Dark Ages, and representing the blackest pages in world history when corruption, violence and treachery prevailed, the commercial practices and customs were undoubtedly vile. The church itself accepted bribes, under one pretense or another, for special privileges. You may, therefore, use your own imagination as to the moral caliber of those who could qualify to become a factor in the service of the great prince, in money-lending transactions with his slaves, peasants, and tenants. The Jews who acted for these princes as collectors of tribute and taxes, of necessity, had to be of such caliber, and it was by the acts of these miscreants that the populace got their impression of Jews. The masses hardly ever came into contact with the feudal master, the duke, or count, or prince, or cardinal. The gentry conveniently stayed in the background, sometimes even screened by anonymity. The hand that held the whip and administered the lashes was that of the Jew. So far as the peasantry was able to see, it was the will of the Jew that imposed starvation, sickness, and misery. A vivid picture of such relationship is given in Lion Feuchtwanger's classic *Jud Süss* (English title *Power*). Incidentally, in the tragic end of this novel, one also gets a glimpse of the final reckoning for the services of such a Jew.

By now we should begin to sense basic reasons for anti-Semitism —why the masses are so steeped in hatred of the Jew. But, you may say, this, too, happened a long time ago, just like the crucifixion story. Since those days, long past, a great many things have happened. Guilds were formed. Then they passed into oblivion, and the industrial age came in. As the big cities grew and developed, capitalism was born and matured. But the identity of the Jew with the role assigned to him many centuries ago, is still fuel for the race-hater.

Here is another masterpiece, written by one who knew Jewish life and character and understood the Jewish scene of the past two centuries. His name is I. J. Singer, and his book is *Brothers Ashkenazi*. The scene is largely laid in Lodz, Poland. The book has five principal characters, which may be said to represent composite Jewry. There is a fairly well-to-do Jewish merchant, decent, respectable, dignified, an upholder of the fine Jewish tradition and character. He has two sons. The older one is ambitious, pushing, grasping, wholly unscrupulous, while the other is the

[14]

exact opposite. Somewhat of an aesthete, the younger brother loves life, is candid, forthright, and radiates happiness, and is not interested in becoming a great financial tycoon like his older brother. Then, there is an old rabbinical teacher, a strong character, unyielding, fanatically orthodox, reminiscent of the old Prophets. He is willing to be tested by his convictions and take the consequences. His son, a radical and a labor leader, is also unbending and willing to pay the price for his beliefs. These five become involved in a complicated web of circumstances, in which each plays to the end the role assigned to him. The older of the two brothers is the villain of the story and brings ruin to all of them and finally to himself. The significant point is that, of the five, the tycoon is the only one to deal with the non-Jewish world. Yet, he is looked upon by those seeking to condemn, as a representative of Jewry, to those people. The millions of Jews who are artisans, artists, mechanics, teachers, scientists, doctors, philosophers are overlooked, and the Jew is pointed up as the man in business. This is taken a step farther; the hate-monger can distort economics to give him the blame for the high cost of living, or inferior quality of the commodity sold. This was the Hitler theme that launched the fallacy of the "Jewish Internationalist."

You can fill many books with illustrations proving this point. But let us take just one: Today the almost universal housing shortage is keenly felt and much discussed. Costs are from two to two-and-a-half times what they were a decade ago and are beyond the reach of the average family. The reason for it is no mystery. The landowners boost their prices; the manufacturers of materials fatten on inordinate profits; labor demands and gets from two to three times the former wages for a day's work, and turns out less work. So it goes all along the line. Jews are now strongly represented in the real estate business in the principal cities, that is, in production, sale, and promotion. Yet they do not control land values, nor the materials market, nor labor, nor the banks or other financial institutions that fix the terms and conditions for loans, nor the insurance companies which make the loans. Yet the average buyer or renter blames the man who offers the house for sale or rent for the excessive cost—and frequently that man is a Jew. I do not mean to whitewash the realty speculator of responsibility for the high cost of housing. He, too, does not miss a trick to pad his pockets. In fact, he has contributed some new tricks involving gouging and, in the case of business

[15]

properties, insists on the basic rent, plus a sliding scale of bonuses contingent on the volume of business the tenant does. He thus forces the tenant to share his profits with him without taking any of the risks. But the point is that, in addition to these sins, the public blames him also for all sins antecedent to him and committed by others. Much the same situation frequently prevails with respect to other essentials, such as food, clothing, amusements, and so on, all down the line.

There is still another quirk in human nature that does not help to improve the attitude and the relations between Jewish and non-Jewish merchants, as well as the consumer generally. The alertness, quickness, originality and resourcefulness of the Jewish brain, especially as pertains to commerce, is well recognized. He senses a "tendency" or "drift" in business long before his non-Jewish rival is even aware of it. That is only natural. Did not the Jew have at least a thousand years' start on the non-Jew? Still, it is equally natural for the non-Jew to be irritated. He does not, of course, admit superiority of mind or skill in the Jew, but finds other reasons that do not entail any element of inferiority. He cannot understand how it happens that where only yesterday he was the fellow on top—well entrenched, superior in education, manners, position, looking on the newcomer with a friendly but patronizing air—and then, as if by magic, he is outdistanced and outwitted. By whom is he outwitted—but by the very refugee of yesterday, a fellow with an atrocious accent and a foreign visage! He ascribes it usually to dubious methods. Sometimes, these methods are dubious, but he overlooks the fact that he and his forebears were the ones who fixed the rules of the game and the newcomer played according to these rules. Occasionally, he charges him with violating the rules, but does nothing to alter the fundamentals that encourage such violation.

Then, let us not forget that in periods of economic stress and strain, when the spotlight of publicity and exposure of the get-rich-quick stunts of the big monopolistic octopus gets too hot, the successful newcomers make good targets to divert attention from others. Then, you soon find, as if out of a clear sky, new subversive movements sprouting like mushrooms. Some of these are: The Sentinels of the Republic; the Silver Shirts, organized by William Dudley Pelley; Defenders of the Christian Faith, by Gerald B. Winrod; the Black Legion, an offshoot of the Ku Klux Klan, and similar organizations. Here again, the Jew is in his ancient and traditional role of world's scapegoat.

SOME PANACEAS

"Very well," the reader may exclaim in a somewhat disheartened tone of voice, "you have made out your case and furnished a bill of particulars, as the lawyers would say. Now, what is the solution? What answer do you offer or what nostrum do you prescribe?"

Before tackling this task, I want to mention some nostrums that have been and are being tried, but have failed.

1. The first may be labeled the "chosen people" complex, the Biblical heritage, the claim that the Jews are the favorite of God Almighty. This, and the second on this list, imply that Jews are better, superior to all other peoples. It does not help relations of the Jews with other people, and it is just insufferable conceit. Besides, it is silly. The fact that practically all other races have at one time or another made the same claim is no excuse for the Jew to continue it.

2. The second is the "mission" complex, or the claim that God has picked us as the ones to improve and uplift all mankind. This claim was trumpeted aloud by the rabbis of the reform temples as an answer to the Zionists, who claimed that the re-establishment of Palestine and nationhood is our *raison d'être*. Like the first nostrum, this, too, is presumptuous and childish and does not do us any good.

3. The third is the perpetual grudge against the Christians that they have never fully appreciated our gift to them of their religion, God, Jesus and Mary, the apostles and the saints, all of whom were Jews. The implication is that they owe the Jew a great debt, which they refuse to discharge. Suppose this is so. Does a people have the right to draw on an account established by its ancestors nineteen hundred years ago? If Einstein had stopped after giving the world the theory of relativity, he would have been acknowledged as a great scientist and benefactor, but he would hardly have kept on reminding the world of this and

dunning it for what he had done. On the contrary, he never slackened his activities for mankind.

Far from getting any immunity or surcease from persecution, some of the most outrageous attacks on the Jew by Christians were made in the very name of the religion and God established by a Jew. Either way, it is idle to continue to expect laurels when it only brings more rebuff. If it is intended to remind the Christian world that the Jew is entitled to better treatment because the Christian world adopted the bible of the ancient Jewish world and their Redeemer and their saints were ancestors of the Jews, then such a position is very humiliating. The Jewish claim to equal rights is based, or should be, on the fact that they are civilized people, contributing to society. It should not be based on what the Jewish ancestors did nineteen hundred years ago. Why, pray, pursue such unbecoming tactics? The simple fact is that the average intelligent non-Jew, with any historical discernment, is fully aware of the overwhelming contribution made by the Jew and does not have to be reminded of it. The predominance of the Jewish mind in the development of religion, ethics and commerce, is uncanny. Christianity itself springs from the Jews. The so-called capitalist order, with its involved and extended banking organizations, its industrial systems, with its department stores, chain stores, and many other ramifications, is largely the product of the Jewish brain. Finally, socialism, destined to revolutionize and replace these contributions of the Jewish mind and now spreading with breathless speed throughout the world, is surely the fruit of Jewish intellect.

Against these indisputable facts, what performance can the Christian world show in the building up of civilization? They can point to their unquestioned superiority in the art of militarism and war-making, which have bred brutality and brought devastation throughout the ages. They can also point to such colossal achievements as the Crusades, the great Inquisition of the Middle Ages, the long era of slavery throughout Europe, known as the Feudal System, and the series of religious wars.

Let these facts speak for themselves and let the Jew be spared the vulgarism of endlessly shouting from the rooftops that he is the darling of God.

4. A fourth bad practice the Jew has fallen into is always to carry a chip on his shoulder and to cry wolf (anti-Semitism), on the slightest provocation. There are times when even the most

sincere non-Jewish friends and well-wishers would like to call the Jews' attention to the mistakes they make, which result in injury to themselves. But they are reluctant to do so, because of the cry that will be raised of anti-Semite. By this time, the Jew should know how to distinguish between friend and foe and have the courage to listen to well-intentioned, constructive criticism. Moreover, only too often, when some Jews get into trouble with the law or have private differences with non-Jews, they start shouting that it is anti-Semitism, and persecution! An outstanding, even if outdated, illustration is the instance when one of the Guggenheims, a family of copper magnates, had a feud with Theodore Roosevelt, then President of the United States, and started calling him an anti-Semite, implying persecution, when he, Guggenheim, actually took very little interest in Jewish problems at that time. Of course, Theodore Roosevelt was too good a politician to be an anti-Semite. It was just name-calling and a form of self-defense by Guggenheim, at the expense of the entire Jewish people; he did a great disservice to his race. This sort of thing is attempted only too often and should be discouraged.

5. Another nostrum resorted to is in the form of sermons from the pulpit, platform, and the press, exhorting Jews to elevate their moral tone and avoid the practices which bring discredit and embarrassment. This is all to the good, but it is as ineffective as church sermons on Sunday. Suggestions are also made to encourage Jews to cease overcrowding the popular professions and the mercantile field by taking up manual trades and farming. That, too, is futile, for the average person, whether Jew or Christian, will choose the vocation he thinks he is best fitted for, or which circumstances make it possible for him to choose.

It is an eternal truism that ease, wealth, and luxury weaken the moral fiber of a people. Jews are no exception. The deterioration in character among them is most alarming. The role played by many Jews in the gambling world and the tie-up, too, in nefarious political and commercial schemes, is most disheartening. But bad as that is, it probably does not result in as much mischief as the bad manners, the vulgarity, and exhibitionism of the nouveau riche.

Some Jewish leaders meet this criticism with a newly coined slogan that Jews are also entitled to their share of criminals and derelicts. That is quite true, but the unpalatable fact is that they just can't afford such a luxury. Enemies and critics are every-

[19]

where quick to take note of the slightest slip-up, the least misdeed of any minorities. The Jewish people are simply not sufficiently entrenched or in sufficient numbers to indulge in a share of miscreants. This may not be deemed a brave position or consistent with constitutional guarantees, but it is a hard and very irritating fact.

The reader may ask: What can be done about it? It may seem to make matters worse by bringing this situation out in the open through public discussion, thereby furnishing grist for the anti-Semitic mill. Ignoring the situation is no better than sweeping the dirt under the carpet or into hidden corners. That you can avoid evil by not looking in the direction whence it stares at you, is dangerous self-deception, not merely in the small and daily facts of life, but also in the realm of mass psychology and social relations. Attempts to cover up or minimize missteps only bring the charge of condoning them. Surgery and antiseptics, no matter how painful, are the only way to treat malignancy. The query may be raised of what is meant by surgery and antiseptics in dealing in human relations. Morally unhealthy human beings cannot be purified and, after that, insulated against all temptations they had succumbed to in the first instance. It is not an easy or simple matter to change overnight the habits of parvenus who have been suppressed all their lifetime and suffered poverty and humiliation and now want to gleefully show off their success in exhibitionism and boasting. There is no simple method to force them to change.

However, psychological analysis does suggest a panacea. Experts on public relations have come to recognize the formidable power of public opinion in molding the thinking and habits of people. The big task is to discover the basic principle of harnessing and marshalling that opinion toward the objective. Here are a few illustrations of patterns of behavior that are common among people. Not so long ago the accepted standard of female beauty, grace, and sex appeal was the well-rounded body, the curve. The tight corset and other devices were worn to bring about such effect, frequently at the price of great discomfort and pain. The bustle was also at one time or another worn to create the same seductive illusion. Then, arbiters and designers of fashion suddenly decreed that the fascinating and magnetic female form must become flat like a pancake. Curves became anathema. Forthwith, there were ushered in not merely new designs and styles (with stays) in garments, but something much more basic. Thousands of women, whose curves were considered only the day before so alluring, went on drastic diets; in many instances this severe dieting had dire health consequences. Some were known to have died as a direct or indirect result of these diets, before the tide again turned in favor of curves. Is this not a striking illustration of the sacrifices at the altar of public opinion?

In a somewhat less grotesque fashion, men, too, suppress their good, hard, common sense, subject themselves to considerable hardship, inconvenience, and expense just to appear popular. They will risk ruin or exposure to imitate a successful rival by "playing the game," in order to merit public admiration or even only approval. It even affects children in a similar way. Several decades ago it was not uncommon to see children of immigrants shy away from their bearded fathers who spoke with foreign accents, because they felt embarrassed. Now many of them, due to the influence of parochial schools, wear religious skull caps and "payelich" in public, to show off the religious influence. All of this demonstrates that what is considered basic and fundamental in human nature will bow to public opinion. From time immemorial, the influence of public opinion on the lives of people in all walks of life has been immeasurable. As these lines are written (March 22, 1951), the press reports of an attempted suicide of a confessed murderer in jail, not because of his impending fate, but because some of the other prisoners jeered at him, calling him a dirty murderer. Thus, even the will to live cannot in some instances withstand public opinion. In sports, many a challenger faces the risk of injury or even death, just for public acclaim.

Hence, it should not be hard to realize that the creation and application of the right kind of public opinion would be a most wholesome and desirable catalysis on the obnoxiously vulgar exhibitionism and manners of upstarts. Today, with wealth revered as the highest human value and attainment, the possessors easily monopolize the attention and admiration of everyone. By comparison, little recognition is now given any other achievement or virtue.

Even in the backward existence of ghetto life under the benighted czars, the virtues of character, refinement and especially erudition were greatly revered. What was termed "yichas" (coming from or being related to people of learning) was a precious commodity in those days. Mere possession of wealth, especially when suddenly acquired and by questionable methods was inadequate for public recognition or position.

What a magnificent and wholesome thing it would be if leaders in public life, the press, and all other agencies for molding public opinion, were to inaugurate an intensive and zealous campaign for self-purification and introspective analysis. Or imagine a Jeremiah rising up and traveling the breadth and length of this great land, and lashing out against the blasphemous homage being paid to the large open purse. One look at reality, and the present set-up will prove what a futile and forlorn hope that is.

When some thousands of years back, the Lord of Hosts, through Moses, gave the Jew a singular honor by picking him for the job of the world's champion whipping-boy in order to disseminate the principles of the Torah, he endowed the Jew with the complex or fixation of "world-saver." He found the Jews a "strange" and "stiff-necked" people, and, indeed, they had to be mighty strange and stubborn for that job. In discharging that mission imposed on them by the Torah as "world-savers," they had to develop great agility for constantly jumping from one extreme to another or, to put it another way, from the fire into the frying pan. The Jews not only invented and developed commerce, banking, and industry, but also gave the world Karl Marx, who thought up Socialism to save the world from the same commerce and capitalism which it gave rise to. His teachings have spread in a short time, as history goes, and have split the world into irreconcilable factions. They are now the greatest and most threatening issues. With characteristic zeal, a great many Jews plunged into the thick of that battle. This zeal was a powerful factor in the frightful punishment meted out to European Jews by the Hitlerites. It is not surprising that the reaction is devastating. Stricken by a great fear, the Jew resorts to a form of atavism and brings back the forms and habits of yesterday, which he fancies will give him security. He thus beckons to old traditions and practices, and, with it, back to chauvinism and the clericalism of the ghetto days. Having more ample means, he is seized by a mania to manifest solidarity and build ramparts of physical protection. These take the form of course of building up the state of Israel and, here, in the diaspora, in erecting a rash of million and multimillion dollar synagogues, temples, and centers. Daily, the Jewish people are confronted by urgent persistent demands for these glamorous and often luxurious houses of worship and other institutions. Are all of them needed? Can they be afforded? Will they be maintained if, and when, the world becomes normal again, and war prosperity comes to an end? In the clamor of pep talks and publicity stunts, dare one ask such questions, much less pose them in public? Have the Jews not given hostages to fate that are bound to plague them in the future?

In this climate of opinion and fortuitous situation, it is no wonder that no one would dream of giving offense to or disturbing the sensibilities of big donors, even when it is known that the source of their wealth is tainted, and that sooner or later their sins will be heaped on all Jews. Can the Jewish people, then, in these circumstances afford a Jeremiah or indulge in introspection or a crusade of self-criticism?

Finding themselves in this dilemma, their very senses of right and wrong have become dimmed. They find themselves under terrific pressure to carry the burdens they assumed were life and death necessities, and now they can ill afford to be discriminating about where the support comes from. As a result, the Jew must lionize those who bring discredit and are a potential menace to his place in the community. How blurred his vision is, and what a contradictory hopeless mess he finds himself in!

CHAPTER IV

LOOKING AHEAD

1

Salvation for the Jew will come when the tempest that is now raging throughout the world comes to an end. This century will be known to posterity as the century of great revolutions and tremendous upheavals in politics, economics, science, and religion. It will either liquidate a great many problems, including the Jewish problem, or it will liquidate civilization, in which case nothing will matter any more.

These upheavals began with the First World War. Among the results of this war was the birth of a premature but lusty political infant in Russia. To its enemies, that creature is a monstrosity; to the more objective realists, it is abnormal and psychopathic. That it developed in this form may be due, in great measure, to the hostility of those who should have been its friends at the start, but who did their best to try to destroy it in its infancy. These early enemies were the status quo sponsors and standpatters. To them, anything new and different is a bugaboo. They still do not know that motion is the essence of life, and that nothing stands still. They fail to recognize that their own pet, the profit system, has grown up, is changing and getting old; in fact, it is creaking badly. Watching it jealously from its beginnings they could not see the changes right under their noses. For instance, if the diet prescribed by their present chief nurse, Robert Taft—such as his housing bill or labor control bill, or the public health bill—had been as much as hinted at thirty or forty years ago, he would have been denounced as a dangerous radical or socialist and have been kicked out. Hence, when that Russian "creature" made its appearance, one look at it was enough to scare them out of their wits, and they became violent. They constantly schemed how to abort and destroy what they regarded as a nightmare. The hysteria soon infected the healthy commercial and social cells throughout Europe, and presently a cancerous growth set in,

[24]

which was soon diagnosed as Fascism. This made some people happy, for they erroneously expected it would attack and destroy the Russian government. It ultimately did attack it, but first it almost destroyed Russia's enemies as well. A dangerous and tragic surgical operation became inevitable. The Second World War saved the world from the cancer, but it nearly destroyed the patient.

The phobias of the two world systems, the old profit system and the new abnormal, crude Soviet system, have come back, with increased hatred and suspicion of each other. Now that the world is still bleeding, starving, and badly in need of a respite and encouragement for the resumption of the huge task of reconstruction, the governments which yesterday fought side by side are threatening each other.

Our own statesmen should by this time understand the evolutionary process of the industrial profit system. They know, or should know, that laissez-faire has ceased to be accepted, particularly by hungry people. The system which started as a small middleman's paradise is now overshadowed by monopoly capital. Monopoly and cartels now rule the roost. To curb them, Government had to step in with regulatory powers, such as the Interstate Commerce Commission, Federal Trade Commission, Securities Commission, the Investment Trust Act and numerous other agencies, especially in times of emergency. Now and then, it has been found necessary for the people, through government, to operate large services and industries, such as parcel post, the TVA, and, in some parts of the world, many other utilities. This government control and government operation has tremendously narrowed the gap that heretofore divided the profit system and socialization of industry. Another factor that makes for the rapid socialization is the fast-growing co-operatives here and abroad. This is a further indication that the highest development of the profit system—indeed, the final stage—leads straight into socialization. This is actually demonstrated by the smooth and easy transition taking place right before our eyes in the socialization of the industries in England.

The Soviet Government, on the other hand, is equally mistaken. The end of the recent war gave it a brilliant opportunity to arrive at an understanding with the Western powers. Former wounds had been healed in the crucible of the worst war in the world's history. It was high time for peace, understanding, and

[25]

reconstruction. Did the Soviet Government, or does it, avail itself of that opportunity? The answer is no. It stirs up old suspicions and antagonisms by a tactless, obstinate, and obdurate attitude. The old Russian Czarist regime fought a war over the Dardannelles and did not get them. Therefore, it became reconciled in doing without a warm-water port. But now, of all times, the Stalin regime feels bound to make an issue of it! Prior to World War II, Russia relinquished its claims on the small Baltic countries, the Polish eastern front, Bessarabia, and portions of Finland. Now that it has these war prizes, it is still not satisfied. It picks issues over the Suez Canal and Iranian oil! It may be in the right about some of these claims. But, is this the time to rock the boat? Her mistake is all the greater, for the trend of events was in Russia's favor. The suffering, distress, and misery everywhere were in themselves enough impetus to make people rebellious, without the Soviet Government intervening to aggravate matters. Then, why can't it be more patient and even generous with its harried allies?

Grim as this impasse between Russia and the capitalist countries is, as fraught as it is with the most dreadful possibilities, it is NOT likely to lead to an armed clash—at least, not for some time. But, whatever happens, the profit system, or so-called private enterprise, is destined, first, to develop into huge monopolies, and ultimately to be socialized. The handwriting is on the wall, in the pattern of the steel, automobile, and oil industries, and the huge apartment building projects promoted by some life insurance companies. There is very little evidence of private enterprise in these industries, in the sense that anyone has a chance to enter these fields with any hope of success. In the automobile and oil industries there are many individuals engaged as sales agents or gas station keepers, but these two huge monopolies fix the terms and conditions of the services. The individuals are, in essence, only glorified employees. In time, that will happen in all other industries. The next inevitable step will be government control, and the final step government operation. All this does not mean violence or civil strife, but transition by evolution.

Some will scoff at these predictions and laugh them off as a pipedream. But, look at Europe! Even the moderate elements, which are opposed to Russia, favor socialization of all industries. On this continent, observing such co-operatives as the Commonwealth Federation of Canada, down to the many co-operatives in

the United States, the labor banks, and similar trends south of
us, you will realize socialization is much closer than you think.
As these lines are written, the American mind is preoccupied with
and greatly disturbed by the international antagonisms between
its government and Russia. Sooner or later, this issue must resolve
itself. If moderation, common sense and a decent concern for
humanity will prevail, some kind of reconciliation and understanding will be arrived at. Then public attention will again turn
toward economic and social betterment. The march toward an
even greater and more perfect "welfare state" will be resumed.
In his monumental book *Inside U.S.A.* (p. 919), John Gunther
says: "The next New Deal will make the last New Deal look mild.
Because, in plain fact, no matter how buttressed up and artifi-
cially stimulated and managed, the free enterprise philosophy is
not working well enough. It is not sufficient."

Now, that means the ultimate disappearance of the middleman,
who now absorbs a big chunk of the cost of commodities. The
retail shopkeeper, the agent, and the broker will go out of existence, as did the horse and buggy with the advent of the automobile. This will automatically rescue the Jew from being always on
the front line as the scapegoat, taking all the blame and bitterness of average Mr. Citizen for his lot under the iniquitous capitalist economy. The fate of the Jewish people under the new dis-
pensation is not cause for their concern. There will be plenty of
need for their talent, skill, ingenuity, and perseverance under
any set-up. But they will be out of the danger zone. They will no
longer be the world's professional scapegoats and shock absorbers.
In his recent book, *Anti-Semite and Jew,* Jean-Paul Sartre elabo-
rates the theme at considerable length to prove that bit by bit
people will emancipate themselves from the curse of racial
prejudices, and anti-Semitism will automatically disappear.

2

There remains one other prolific source of anti-Semitism to be
considered—the religious differences between Jew and Christian.
These however, are secondary, in the opinion of the writer, for if
the argument advanced herein has any validity, the primary
cause is commercial jealousy—the unsavory enterprises which expose the Jew to all sorts of charges. Religious differences, of
course, do not help either, although they now play a secondary

[27]

role in creating friction. For one thing, there are religious differences even inside the ranks of the principal Christian denominations, such as between Catholics and Protestants, Christian Scientists, the Mormon Church, and so on.

However, there are now visible on the horizon signs of a spectacular metamorphosis that will lay the foundation for a universal religion, an ethical and philosophic religion that will contain the essence of the best in all religions. The Unitarians, the Universalist churches, the Ethical Culture movement, though small, have made a conspicuous beginning and, in many respects, the Quakers have always followed this direction. Thus, the Unitarians proclaim: "Unitarian churches are dedicated to progressive transformation and ennoblement of individual and social life, through religion, in accordance with advancing knowledge and the growing vision of mankind. Bound by this common purpose, and committed to freedom of belief, Unitarians hold in unity of spirit a diversity of convictions." (American Unitarian Association, 1942.) Morever, the advance guard of Unitarianism repudiates the divine origin of Jesus, the Holy Trinity, and the rest of the supernatural beliefs and practices of the church. They deny the theory of an anthropomorphic deity and practically adopt the pantheism of Spinoza. That opens the door to a religion of universal acceptance, in place of the present denominations that promote opposition to each other and create a much divided human race. The substitution of a universal type of religion, in place of the many present benighted predatory religions, with their thickly encrusted covering of superstition and hostility toward one another, cannot by any stretch of the imagination be considered a surrender of one antiquated religion for another no less antiquated. It is definitely not assimilation in the old sense of conversion to the Christian faith. It is a coalescence and refinement of all the old religions.

At the present time, the American Jewish community contains within it a large body of younger rabbis of ability, intellect, imagination, and potential leadership. No group was ever better equipped and poised to take up the challenge to lead their people into a world of universal brotherhood and understanding. Many of them try to do it now, to the limited degree permitted under present day handicaps of diverse cliques and factions. Free of these shackles, they can become the spiritual and intellectual leaders of mankind.

With the acceptance of a rational, higher order of universal theology, and freed from the scapegoat function in the economic and political sphere, the Jew will cease to be the world's "sore thumb." He will feel, and be, the equal of anyone. As was so well said by Julian Morgenstern, former president of Hebrew Union College: "The Jew will ultimately cease to play the role of a distinct, racial national group, and the descendants of the Jews today will be recognized and will recognize themselves only as Americans." (*Contemporary Jewish Record*, Vol. V, p. 143, 1942.)

In the past decade, Americans have become quite race-conscious. In addition to the perennial anti-Semitism and the Negro problem, they have had the Neisi (American-born Japanese) problem on the West coast during the recent war. Public interest is manifested by discussions of race problems in the daily and periodical press and public forums. A number of books on the subject have also made their appearance in the last few years. Among these are *Anatomy of Racial Intolerance*, by George de Huszar (1946), and *Glass House of Prejudice*, by Dr. Dorothy Baruch (1946). There are also two other books more directly concerned with anti-Semitism: *Essay on Anti-Semitism*, edited by Koppel S. Pinson (1946), and *Anti-Semitism a Social Disease*, edited by Ernst Simmel (1946). These four books contain case histories, anthologies, as well as psychological and philosophical explorations into and interpretations of minority and race antipathies.

A later and more matter-of-fact treatment of the subject is presented by Carey McWilliams in *A Mask for Privilege* (1948). The style and content of this book are more in the nature of a lawyer's brief than an objective exploration of the subject. The book is, however, helpful in answering many of the stock arguments against Jews. Add to the literature on the subject, the Jewish and inter-faith organizations to combat anti-Semitism, and one gets a bird's-eye-view of the battle lineup between the Jew and his critics.

In this brief essay on anti-Semitism, I have tried to present what I regard as the salient factors of the problem, without the irrelevancies, diatribes, self-pity or rhetorical philippics that characterize most of the utterances of Jewish leaders in dealing with this subject. However, here and there I have hinted gently that perhaps the Jew, too, is to blame. It would be of great help to the Jews in their struggle to look about them and see to what extent some of them furnish grist for the mill that spews the anti-Semitic poison.

It must be obvious that for a layman to start a much needed wholesome cleansing process or inquiry to improve the behavior of some of the Jews would in the first place be self-defeating and only invite a great deal of abuse and recrimination against him. But it is high time for Jewish leadership, particularly the spiritual leaders who are charged with moral guidance, to display more courage in the direction of self-criticism and introspection. Too many, as in the days of the ancient Prophets, are content to protect their fleshpots and leave the unpleasant tasks of criticism to the abused and greatly misunderstood Prophets. True, these times, when the Jewish people are surrounded by so many traducers and enemies, may be too dangerous to indulge in the luxury of housecleaning. Yet, the ancient Prophets also lived through hazardous periods when their brethren dwelled in the dens of wolves and beasts, but they did not hesitate to apply moral disinfectants to avoid putrefaction.

3

An appropriate conclusion to this chapter is the following, culled from an article in the *Jewish Floridian* of January 26, 1945, by George Talianoff, Executive Director, Anti-Defamation League. In this, he quotes a summary of the findings of four well-known psychiatrists and psychologists on anti-Semitism, at an open forum of social scientists held in San Francisco, in January, 1945:

1. Anti-Semitism is not a sporadic phenomenon, as many like to think. On the contrary, it has a continuous history of twenty centuries or more. There may be some question as to how the virus originated but there is no question that the bias is firmly rooted as a tradition in Western civilization.
2. The prejudice is directed not against any particular segment of Jewry but against Jewry in general—against the well-to-do and the poor—against the cultured and the ignorant—against the assimilated as well as the ghettoized. Anti-Semitism is a hatred or dislike not so much of particular Jews as of the abstract concept, "the Jew."
3. The modes of transmission of indoctrination from generation to generation are many, but generally the bias is developed in early childhood. It may be the attitude toward Jews expressed in the home through

cynical or derogatory references, it may be the result of early religious teachings, it may be a reflection of attitudes of other children.

4. Depending on the nature of the influence, anti-Semitism may be a conscious hate or is more likely to be a dislike embedded in the subconscious as one grows into adulthood. Whether this comes into play later as an active force, and the extent of its virulence in a particular individual, depend on such factors as the other civilizing influences to which one has been exposed, and to such environmental conditions as the general economic situation, a war.

5. Although anti-Semitism is not actually caused by bad times, by war, by occupational mal-distribution of Jews, by professional or business competition, etc., these conditions, inasmuch as they result in personal frustrations, in a sense of guilt, do enable the demagogues to stir subconscious prejudices into life against the classic psychological scapegoat, the Jew.

6. We are told by our scientists that the effect of anti-Semitism on the individual Jew is often developed as compensatory emotional reactions or patterns, e.g., to withdraw, to become over-aggressive, etc., and this in turn increases anti-Semitism, making a vicious circle.

The moderator summarized these scientists' recommendations for treatment as follows:

Recognizing the imperative necessity for all that is being done by civic protective agencies, recognizing that Jews themselves can by certain measures reduce the areas of irritation somewhat, granting that psychiatry can accomplish a great deal by giving individuals insight, nevertheless we must at the same time strive towards fundamental correction, (a) by improving environmental conditions to aid the maintenance of world peace, etc., tensions and frustrations, e.g., by providing a healthy economic milieu, by the maintenance of world peace, etc.; (b) by broad social programming to minimize the original implantation of preconcerted prejudice, and wide-scale participation by such major social institutions as the home, the church and the school.

In describing the program as a "Herculean task," the moderator concluded:

But they must be attempted and carried through. Careful studies show that the United States is perhaps more vulnerable than ever before, that eighty-five per cent of our people are today ready to make scapegoats of one group or another in our heterogeneous population. And racial and religious prejudice can spread like a prairie fire. The American public must be awakened to realize that what is at stake is the democratic principle itself, the essence of which is respect for the individual, the toleration of differences, and social justice.

[31]

PART TWO

CHAPTER I

ISRAEL AND THE DIASPORA

Assuming that the birth pains of young Israel will soon be over and a "modus vivendi" reached with the neighboring and domestic Arabs, the American Jewish community will be faced with one of the most momentous issues in its entire history. Indeed, Jewish communities throughout the Diaspora will be faced with varying aspects of the same issue. What will be the psychological and spiritual attitude of the segment of Jews in Israel—who, from the standpoint of the nationalists, are the soul, head, and heart of world Jewry—to the mass of Jews in the rest of the world? That the present numerical ratio may change slightly in favor of Israel will not materially lessen the disproportion. At best, the Jewish world body will still remain a monstrosity, a very much inflated brain with an elongated, shapeless body. A second important issue will be the legal and economic relationship between Jewish communities in the Diaspora and the Israeli government.

For the present and during the ecstatic honeymoon period, these questions may not appear of great moment, but with the advent of daily practical problems and difficulties, they will loom larger and larger. The greatest optimists of today realize that under the most favorable circumstances the new Jewish State will for many years have to lean heavily on the Jews in the Diaspora, and most heavily on American Jews. Will the Jewish community here be satisfied to contribute a great deal of money without having some say about the handling and disposition of it? Will the Jewish people here be contented with just a condescending and sometimes contemptuous nod? True, the officials and the rank and file among American Zionists now disclaim any intention of interfering in any manner with the sovereign rights of Israel. Yet, only recently, even prior to the proclamation of the Jewish State, a heated dialectic conflict was raging between American and Israeli Zionists, concerning certain jurisdictional rights and the ratio of representation. Indeed, the controversy was waxing hot when other developments intervened to take their minds off the issue. But it is bound to reappear again and again.

Of even greater complexity will be the more subtle human elements of pride, dignity, and moral attitudes, which can best be expressed by the recently coined word "psychocultural." It springs from the dizzy heights to which Israeli Jews have been raised and rhapsodized about by their brother Jews in the Diaspora. Just as Chaim Bialik, who is reported to have said that one Jew in Palestine is worth ten of the Galut, Zionists have vied with one another in their obsequiousness and humility toward their brethren in Eretz Israel. Professor Israel Knox, in an article in *Commentary*, August, 1948, p. 114, reports that a young rabbi shouted at a gathering: "The Jews of Palestine have status and dignity; the Jews of the Galut have no status and no dignity!" And Dr. Emanuel Neumann, one time president of the Zionist Organization, refers to the Jews here in the United States as Galut Jews. Dr. Samuel Margoshes, editor of a prominent Jewish daily in New York City, and a pioneer Zionist leader, declaims in an editorial (*Day*, June 25, 1948): "What is there in American Jewish life of today to fire one's imagination? Time was when the immigrant to these shores, with not a cent in his pocket but a boatload of dreams of the American promise, made excellent copy for sentimental novelists. But the heroic pioneering days are over, and the universal grayness, which is the predominant color of the American Jewish scene, has very little, indeed, to attract attention. If there is anything in American Jewish reality to strike the fancy of the American Jewish youth, it must have missed it." It is, indeed, a far cry from the eulogies of Americanism by Mary Antin and others, a half century ago, or by Israel Zangwill in his play, *The Melting Pot*.

The corollary to this change of front and the self-abasement implied in the suggestion that the handful of Jews in Eretz Israel are the cream and those in the United States hardly good enough to be skimmed milk, gives rise to a second query: What is the general status and position of the great majority of Jews throughout the Diaspora, and that of the Jews here in the United States? Are the Jews here merely a kite to the newly-born State in Palestine, or do they have some purpose, function, and responsibility aside from the role assigned to them in the Bible?

The answer to this question brings to mind an ancient legend, which I think comes from the Midrash. Put somewhat irreverently, it goes like this: The Lord of Hosts (God) canvassed the nations to try to get one of them to accept His Torah, but none would have it. He finally approached His chosen tribe of Israel, and, through Moses, said in effect: "Yisroleck, it's up to you. I have a very precious thing in the Torah; the world needs it. Either you accept and assume all the burdens under it, or you will be buried under this mountain (Mount Sinai). Make your choice." So they did.

The rabbis of old and the modern chauvinists have lulled the Jews into the belief that their sole function in this world, their chief reason for existence, is to coddle the Torah in its pristine purity, and, at any cost, to re-establish and maintain a State in Palestine, in order to be able to project from there the Messianic mission imposed on them by the Torah. Their own secular and natural requirements, personal hopes, aspirations, and ambitions are to be subordinated and sublimated to that task. Their very lives thus play second fiddle to the overtowering ambition to indoctrinate and impress on the rest of the world a code, a body of principles and dogmas, sealed against change or amendment some two thousand years ago.

This writer identified himself with political and economic Zionism the better part of his life, feeling that Jews are entitled to a haven of refuge and a political status. These, as he understood it, were the principal motives that goaded men like Moses Hess, Theodore Herzl, Max Nordau, and Israel Zangwill in their labors for the cause. That a clear-cut endemic Jewish culture would inevitably follow the realization of a Jewish State would be all to the good and a desirable concomitant to the main goal of national security and dignity. Palestine was, of course, the first, but not the only choice. Inasmuch as the main objective was to rescue Jewry from persecution and the Ghetto, any place offering the prospect of a viable, independent state would have to do, if Palestine proved unattainable. That this was the attitude of the early founders of Zionism was certainly manifest in Zangwill's ITO movement as well as Herzl's attitude at the Sixth Basle Congress. This was not so with the Bible Zionists. With them, it was from the very start, "Palestine or Bust!" They were set to smash every effort at establishing Jewish political independence outside of Palestine. Their antagonism and hostility toward even such partial political status as in the Jewish Colonies in the Ukraine and the Crimea proves it.

Happily, it would appear that for the present the issue over Palestine is closed. Little tolerance is shown for dissidents. On the Jewish scene today there is apparently no room for anyone who regards himself as a secular Jew, a non-conformist—much less an agnostic—who, loving his people, is anxious to co-operate with them in all problems affecting their social, political, and economic status, without subscribing to the religious and chauvinistic dogmas that are the order of the hour. The present Jewish religious and secular leadership has managed to wrap up a neat bundle of parochial Judaism, containing ritual and old traditions plus a dose of chauvinism, and to present it to the rationalist or non-conformist Jew with a "take-it-or-leave-it" attitude.

What such a Jew would like to have answered is this: Did God create the Jewish people, give them the Torah, and bid them set up the capital in Jerusalem, for His own edification and glory as a sort of divine whim? Or is the Torah and the Jewish religion intended as a guide and means to safeguard, promote, and secure their welfare and happiness right here in this earthly existence? If this second hypothesis is correct, is it not the right and duty of Jews to pattern and adjust their theology and ethical imperatives so that they will promote, and contribute to their welfare, happiness, peace of mind and security, regardless of ancient dogmas and precepts to the contrary? In other words, are the Jews here in this world to sustain the dicta of a religion, or is their religion intended to sustain them in their struggles? Was it not the intent of a benevolent Lawgiver to lead and guide their ancestors from the sands of a wild desert of ignorance and helplessness into the light of knowledge, enlightenment, self-help, and dignity, as the successive generations evolved and grew to mental maturity?

I do not charge the present generation of rabbis, nor those of yesterday, with having cast their religious concepts and practices into a straitjacket. The unbending rigidity and complexes of their orthodoxy are a form of atavism—a throw-back of some twenty centuries. It was then that the two, the Torah and Palestine, were fused into one and became the core of Jewish existence, growing into an *idée fixe*. As the "Zohar" puts it: "God, Israel, and the Torah are one."

In this respect the Jews differ from other ancient peoples.

Let us see how and why that came about.

CHAPTER II

NOSTALGIA FOR PALESTINE

The early recorded histories of nations began in nebulous forms of myth and legend, such as the Greeks with the adventures of Helen of Troy, and the Romans with Romulus and Remus. In time, these tales became part of the folklore and literature of their countries and the themes for other forms of art. Some of these were later tied in by the Christians with their religion, the source of which was Jewish; but in the main they regarded these tales with good-natured pride and amusement. This was not so with the Jews. Their myths and legends became part of the heart and core of the Bible and were thereby sanctified and enshrined by all believers, either as Holy Writ or transformed into ritual. Of immeasurably greater effect was another feature of the Bible, which is unique. While God makes the Jews his chosen people, He does not give them the sovereignty of His immense earth, as well He might, but promises them, during good behavior, a miserly tiny space, a mere dot, one might say, on the globe's surface, specifically Canaan, a part of modern Palestine. Concerning that meager spot, He left not the slightest doubt, as can be seen from the following quotations: "And I am come down to deliver them out of the hands of the Egyptian and to bring them up out of that land unto a good land and a large, unto a land flowing with milk and honey." (Exodus, Chapter 3:8) "Now the Lord had said unto Abram, 'Get thee out of thy country and from thy kindred, and from thy father's house, unto a land I will show thee.' " (Genesis, Chapter 12:1) More by emphasis and by iteration and reiteration, it becomes the very core, the *raison d'être* of the Jews as a people. It seems that the whole purpose and objective of the Jewish people, individually and as a nation, is that they occupy that strip of territory and maintain a temple for the edification and glory of God. That theme is woven into the very woof and fiber of the Jewish mentality. It permeates its entire religious culture and literature and much of its civil and material life. There even grew up a legend that God first created the Torah, and then the world and man so that they could keep the Torah.

What accounts for this extraordinary emphasis? Where is there a parallel to it? It might have been due to a strong nostalgia for Palestine, amounting to a passion on the part of the early writers of the Bible. But how account for it after a lapse of twenty centuries?

Describing Palestine as a land of milk and honey is just another manifestation of this partiality. It never was that and is not today, when so many other countries have been discovered and settled. One description of it is as follows: "Almost the entire southern half of Israel is a hot, waterless desert, the Negev, with temperatures running up to 110 degrees. A large part of the rest of the country is also a wasteland, neglected for almost 2000 years." (*Atlantic Monthly,* April, 1951, p. 4) Egypt was in fact in Biblical days the bread-basket of the several countries surrounding it, as is borne out by the fact that on two occasions the early Hebrews went there in quest of food—once by Abraham, when he made the classical faux pas by insisting that Sarah, his wife, pose as his sister, and the second in the days of Jacob, when he, with his family, went there during another famine. One wonders why an all-powerful deity, such as Yahweh insisted He was, could not have promised Egypt to the early Jews—a gift much more befitting His dignity and that of His chosen people!

Be that as it may, Canaan became an *idée fixe* and remained an obsession to the generations of patriarchs and all succeeding generations to this day. The longing for *Eretz Yisroel* (Land of the Jews) was inculcated into the very physical and spiritual being of the Jew. It is integrated into his religion, his prayers on all holidays, and on secular days. He is not permitted to forget it during his feasts, for every wish on every possible occasion includes it, and the termination of his high holidays winds up with "Leshona-Abu-Be-Yerishalayim" (next year in Jerusalem).

It is true that for decades and ages this Jerusalem complex became more or less of a perfunctory and spiritless formality, and the Jews became apathetic, especially during those long interludes when its realization was regarded as impossible or very remote. Aside from the role played by Palestine as the early homeland of the Patriarchs and the tribes, the Jews occupied it as a nation during two extensive periods. The first dated from somewhere in the 12th century to 586 B.C., during which time they were buffeted and kicked around like a football between the Egyptian, Syrian, Babylonian, and Median Empires, the Great Powers of that part of the world then. By 516 B.C., the second temple was completed, and Judea maintained its precarious existence as a political entity until the tragic destruction of the second temple by Titus in 72 B.C., and the exile that followed. Neither of these relatively long periods of Jewish statehood were an undiluted sovereign bliss. The age-old tragedy was and is today that Palestine was the crossroads of a clashing, rumbling civilization. Ezekiel called Jerusalem "the door of the nations," and he did not mean the weak nations. When someone else controls the door to your home, it cannot be said to be your home exclusively.

Still another important fact is that at no time did all of the Jews in the world abide in Palestine. During most of pre-exilic Jewish history, according to the best authorities, there were more Jews in the Diaspora of the pre-Christian era than lived in and around Palestine. Philo claims that in his own time about a quarter of a million Jews lived in the delta of the Nile. In *Readers Digest,* of September, 1949 (p. 57), Dr. Abba Hillel Silver claims that in the latter part of the sixth century of the Christian Era, there were about two and a half million Jews living in Palestine and five and a half million outside of Palestine.

It is true that the large Jewish communities outside and away from Palestine looked to Jerusalem for spiritual guidance and leadership, very much as present-day Catholics in the United States look to the Vatican in Rome. But in their civil, political, and social lives they were part of the nation or people among whom they lived, sharing their good or bad fortune. The prevailing civilization and culture in those countries where the Jews lived outside of Palestine was Hellenic, and thus was first introduced the great Hellenic schism among the Jews. On the other hand, the Jews who lived in Palestine, aside from their political difficulties with neighboring nations, also had their internal struggle. There were rich and poor Jews, leftists and rightists, liberals, conservatives, venal politicians, and at times their public officials and even the clergy were corrupt. The Prophets bear witness to all that.

From all this it must be evident that for those times, and given the peculiar conditions which always did surround Palestine in relation to the countries bordering it, the Jews did not lead too happy a political life. However, it was not unlike that of other peoples who inhabited the country prior to the coming of the Jews, and those who occupied it since their exile. It is therefore not easy to understand the religious and nostalgic tenacity that characterizes their claim to Palestine today. As indicated above, the main reason for it is probably the psychological one that made Zion the pivotal point around which the religious edifice was built, and the one thus became inseparable from the other.

However, even this tie would in time have loosened and disappeared had the Christian world adopted a normal, decent, and civilized attitude toward the Jews; but those were neither decent nor civilized times. Not long after the Jews were driven out of Zion, the Dark Ages set in. In the opinion of many competent students of history, backed by many historical facts, the church was the greatest setback to civilization in that era, from which it has not yet recovered completely. That was visually and physically demonstrated by the savagery of the Christian hordes during the crusades, in contrast with the more human behavior of the Saracens whom they attacked, and who were then the bearers of pagan civilization. It is true that since then, for reasons too intricate to be gone into here, the Mohammedans and other Near-Eastern and Far-Eastern peoples took a tailspin in a backward direction, while the Christian nations made tremendous forward leaps in culture, art, and particularly in the physical sciences. However, that was merely on the surface; actually, their barbarism only took on different forms. Otherwise, there was little, if any, mitigation.

This is shown on the pages of history by a consistent and ever-rising tradition of wars and human slaughter. The leaders of this tradition are the same who were so formidable centuries ago— the Teutons. It is, therefore, easy to understand the savage treatment and persecution of the Jews by the Christian nations right from the beginning of the Christian era and continuing in one form or another down to the present day. These persecutions were integrated with the religious complex the Jews evolved for Zion and independence, and gave them the strong determination to regain the homeland. That inflexibility rose and fell as the periodic persecution crises fluctuated. If persecution increased, the desire to throw off the foreign yoke was intensified; it flagged when persecution decreased. On some occasions when the pressure became unbearable, the Jews were driven to desperate measures. History discloses three such notable instances. The first was a brilliant epic in Jewish history—the famous rebellion and military exploits of the Maccabees, memorialized by the celebration of Hanukah (165-142 B.C.). Actually, however, it was more a clash between Judaism and Hellenism. The second was a complete and terribly tragic fiasco for the Jews. That, too, had its inception in interference with the religious practices of the Jews, similar to the cause of the Maccabean revolt. This time it was against the Roman King Hadrian. The spiritual head of the Jewish community was the celebrated Rabbi Akiba, who bestirred the military genius Bar Kochba to lead the revolt. But the odds were against him, and, after some initial triumphs, the revolt was suppressed with the loss of close to half a million lives.

The third great misfortune to befall Jewry was the most bizarre hoax that ever happened to a people, the greatest tragi-comedy on the stage of history. "Shabbtai-Zweenik," a corruption of "Shabbathai-Zebi," is to this day the synonym for faker or charlatan. It all happened in the middle of the 17th century, when Europe had been wasted and ruined by the Thirty Years' War, and the Jews, besides being embroiled in the general suffering, had had a Hitlerian nightmare in the Chmielnicki uprisings. Chmielnicki was really the prototype of Hitler, and for his day did a real job of torturing and massacring the Polish Jews. In short, all of Europe, and particularly the Jews, were so demoralized by suffering and despair that they were ready and anxious to believe anyone or anything that offered any relief or comfort from their intolerable misery. Shabbathai, who lived in Smyrna, was deeply sunk in cabalism, and today would be classified as a psychopath. He announced that he was the Messiah and was prepared to rescue the Jews from exile and place the "kingdom of the world" in their hands. Many in Smyrna began to believe in him, and the agitation took possession of the entire Jewish community and nearly disrupted it; for others recognized him as a faker and considered him as a menace. Finally, he was driven out of Smyrna, but he took to traveling eastward, making converts and followers.

Presently, the movement spread like wildfire. Wonders and miracles began to be credited to him by his followers. These were described with monstrous distortions, as word passed from mouth to mouth and from city to city throughout Europe, in a day when there was scarcely any other means of communication. Even the

[43]

non-Jewish world sat up and took notice, and it became a topic of interest on the exchanges. Life in the Jewish communities in the East and in Europe became demoralized. Everywhere, it was said the Messiah had come, and the Jews the world over would be triumphantly removed to Jerusalem, from where they would rule the universe. What need, then, of planning and struggling and scheming, or even trying to bother with any business or work, when in a matter of weeks or months at the latest, this great miracle was to take place? Sachar, in his *History of the Jews* (page 243) says Pepys noted in his *Diary* that Jews in London offered 100 pounds to 10 that in two years the princes of the East would crown Shabbathai King of Jerusalem. There began a movement among wealthy Jews to get rid of their establishments and other immovable property. In short, a kind of madness and confusion spread in most Jewish communities. When it was at its height, the Sultan summoned Zebi to his capitol at Constantinople and, after a brief stay there, gave him the choice of conversion to the Islamic faith, or execution. He decided to live and became the Sultan's doorkeeper under the name of Mohammed Effendi. When that news became public, the Jews of Europe were overcome with shame and horror. Their feverish hope for certain redemption turned to frigid despair, but at least they regained their sanity. There have been recurring false Messiah incidents since, with varying doleful consequences, but none so devastating as the one of Shabbathai-Zebi.

CHAPTER III

EVOLUTION OF ZIONISM

Let us now review the events that made Palestine a political reality. As shown above, the Jew's yearning for Palestine was age-old and imbedded in his sub-consciousness. While for centuries it lay dormant, finding an outlet only in his prayers for a return to Palestine, the actual nostalgic pangs for a return to the land of his fathers flared up in him mostly during emergencies, when his lot in Galut became unbearable. "Common sorrow unites man more closely than common joy," said Renan. The Damascus blood libel moved Moses Hess, a prominent German Socialist leader, to turn aside from his interest in the German working class to concentrate on the Jewish problem. The same crisis was also a factor in the creation of the *Alliance Israélite Universelle* by Adolph Cremieux. In 1862, Hess published his famous *Rome and Jerusalem,* which promulgated the historic and economic basis for a Jewish center in Palestine by suggesting a complete scheme for Jewish rejuvenation of the neglected Holy Land through colonization by the Jews. This book moved Graetz, the famous Jewish historian, to exclaim in an article published in 1864: "The Jewish race is approaching under our very eyes a rejuvenescence which would formerly not have been thought possible." He compared this "stirring of the dead bones" with a similar agitation among the exiles in Babylon (*Zionism,* Gottheill, page 38). Some twenty years later the Maskillim, or Jewish liberals in Russia, had a rude awakening from their dream of liberation in the May Laws of 1880 and the pogroms that followed. That stirred one of their leaders, Dr. Leo Pinsker, to write his well-known *Autoemancipation,* in which he reached similar conclusions and suggested the same remedies as Hess, though it is not known that he knew or had heard of *Rome and Jerusalem.* The practical result of these two books and the agitation that followed, was the organization of the "Chovevi-Zion" (Lovers of Zion), which, though wide-spread in the Ghetto, was never to become a world movement.

Then followed the epic of Theodore Herzl, the creator of the present Zionist movement. A picturesque figure, cosmopolitan, not of the Jewish masses like Pinsker, he, too, was stirred by a Jewish tragedy, the Dreyfus Case, which kindled the anti-Semitic inferno throughout France. He, like Hess and Pinsker, set forth his dream of rebuilding Palestine as a refuge and home for Israel in his *Judenstaat,* without apparently having known or heard of the works of either Hess or Pinsker. This effort of his was not accorded a friendly reception, either by his affluent co-religionists or the masses in the Jewish community of the West. But it did attract some notable figures, including Dr. Max Nordau, Israel Zangwill, and the Kadimah Society of Vienna. However, in Eastern Europe where the soil of nationalism had been cultivated and fertilized by the work of the "Chovevi" societies, it received warm and enthusiastic acclaim.

It is to be noted that, at first, neither Hess, Pinsker, nor Herzl advocated more than a civil haven of refuge for Jews under some form of autonomous home rule, guaranteed by a charter they sought and hoped to obtain from Abdul Hamid, then the Sultan of Turkey. Neither were they committed unalterably to Palestine, as testified to by Professor Richard Gottheil, one of the foremost American Zionist leaders, in his authoritative book on Zionism. He says: "Nowhere in his pamphlet (Pinsker's *Autoemancipation*) is the word 'State' used. He speaks of a 'home' and of a 'colonial community' (p. 66). Palestine exercises no fascination upon him (Herzl). . . . It is but one of the various possibilities for Jewish settlement, as is Argentina or Canada. In the *Judenstaat* there are no dithyrambs." (pages 90 and 91) But at the Sixth Zionist Congress in Basle, 1903, after a long wrangle, the Eastern Zionists prevailed, and a declaration was adopted to the effect that "the object of Zionism is to establish for the Jewish people a publicly and legally assured home in Palestine." (*Trial and Error,* by Chaim Weizmann, p. 87)

It is therefore clear that the Zionist founders and early leaders, for historic and sentimental reasons, preferred Palestine, but, if it could not be obtained, the Jews were to turn their eyes to some other part of the world—until this point of view was definitely scrapped by the Basle declaration referred to above.

But how can one account for the fixed idea of Eastern or Russian Zionists that Palestine must be the only spot in the wide world where Jews could find a place of refuge? The answer, in the opinion of this writer, is wholly psychological and calls for a historical flash back to explain it.

In their Ghetto life, the Jews in Russia held their religion and Bible close to their heart. It was an escape from the persecution, suffering, and humiliation they endured from the government, the clergy, and the non-Jewish masses. The privilege of being the "chosen people" and the custodians of the precious Torah served to enable them to bear their burdens and maintain their sanity. Then, in 1855, the heavy clouds broke, and a powerful ray of hope appeared on the horizon. Alexander II came to the Russian throne in a glory of promise and hope. A strong liberal tide set in. The bars against the Jews were let down. Schools and universities were opened to them. Likewise, many economic privileges were extended to them. This was the era when the younger and more enlightened of the Jewish generation were strongly influenced by the intellectual renaissance set in motion by the French Revolution. This enlightenment was not limited to the political and economic levels only; it was also felt strongly in the theological sphere. Darwinism shook the very foundations of religious tradition. Among Jews, the teachings of Leopold Zunz acted as the conveyor-belt to bring these new ideas into the Ghetto. He was aided and abetted by Nachman Krochmal and Solomon Rapoport, who, in turn, were strongly influenced by the teachings of Moses Mendelssohn. Thus the Haskala movement was born. The Jewish people do not do things by halves. They go "whole hog." To those who embraced it, the Haskala meant a break with the past and complete emancipation from old beliefs, traditions, customs, and practices. The neophytes of the new school called themselves Maskillim. Between them and the old generation of fundamentalists a bitter feud broke out. It shook the Jewish world to its foundation, for the polemics and quarrels were only too often intra-family—the young versus the old, son against father. Such contemporary writers as Peretz, Smolenskin, David Frishman, M. L. Lilienblum, and many others were naturally with the young reformers.

Then, like a burst from a modern shell, came the terrible May Laws of 1880, which in one swoop canceled all privileges for the Jews, imposed new disabilities, and ushered in an era of cruel persecutions and pogroms. This was the end of the hopes of the Maskillim, and a vindication of the claims of the fundamentalists. For, the argument ran: Did not the Maskillim preach that the new enlightenment, emancipation, and assimilation with Western culture would ultimately bring freedom from political and cultural discrimination? Well, here is what you got! The position of the Maskillim completely collapsed, and they felt betrayed by the non-Jewish liberals, who failed to come to their aid. At the same time, they could not entirely wipe the slate clean of the mental inroads of the new teachings and resume their status in their Ghetto existence. They could not very well forget the eternal verities they had imbibed in the principles of Darwin, Mendelssohn, Geiger, Krochmal, Rapaport, and others. These new ideas were assimilated and became part of them. They finally found comfort, because of the rebuff from the gentile world, in a deep, desperate, Jewish nationalism. The writings of Hess, Pinsker and others showed them the way out by concentrating their frustrated energies on Jewish settlements in Palestine. They were abetted and guided into this state of mind by the profound intellect of Ahad Ha'am (Asher Ginzberg), a lovable, unobtrusive personality. He was to the Maskillim what Moses Mendelssohn was to the German Jews of the previous century. Each in his time and way was the moral and intellectual mentor to his generation, with this essential difference: Mendelssohn addressed himself to the German people and went forth armed with the Prophets and the Pentateuch, which he rendered into the vernacular, thereby displaying and popularizing the ancient Hebrew heritage. He conceived it as his mission, and that of all Jews as the chosen people, to disseminate the light from the Ark among the nations of the Earth. This doctrine was later to be transmitted to, and become the core of, the Reform Movement in Germany and the United States. Ahad Ha'am, on the other hand, argued for erecting or setting up a great Beacon of light on Mount Sinai or Mount Scopus to illuminate and irradiate all mankind. He was not satisfied with what his people had already achieved, great as that may have been, in the field of metaphysics, ethics, and morals, but wanted them to continue to function from a common center under the aegis of nationalism and with racial consciousness. In this wise, they were to carry aloft the mission of the "chosen people" as the moral mentors of mankind. This, he insisted, must emanate from Palestine. That, Ahad Ha'am maintained, was what was meant by the Messianic prophecy.

This, to my mind, explains why under David Wolffsohn, Chaim Weizmann, and other leaders, the Russian Jewish nationalists fought so strenuously the East Africa or Uganda offer of a Jewish home brought them by Zangwill from the British Government, and why, in the face of support of the Uganda offer by Herzl, they forced the Declaration on Palestine at the 1903 Sixth Basle Congress. However, it would be misleading to claim that all of the disillusioned Maskillim turned to nationalism. Many of them had gone too far to the left to feel happy as Zionists. Quite a large segment joined the political underground as Marxists and revolutionists generally.

But those who turned to nationalism became the backbone of Zionism. They were the most vociferous and dynamic element. Even at that, the movement was in its infancy and weak. With the orthodox Jews—who could only see salvation in the coming of the Messiah—standing aloof and with the richer Western Jews holding on to another philosophy and outlook, and the revolutionary element to still another outlook, there remained but a small segment of the Jewish population in support of the Zionist point of view. What added to the weakness of the Zionists was the fact that while they knew where they wanted to go, they did not have the faintest idea how they could get there. Poor Herzl went peddling his idea to the Courts of Europe, spending years just to get a royal audience without accomplishing anything. He presented the picture of a modern Don Quixote, charging against windmills. His own people, those of influence and wealth, ridiculed the idea as Utopian and impractical. He succumbed under this heavy load of failure and disillusionment.

Thus, Zionism lingered on until there came a totally unforeseen dramatic event in the world's history: the First World War and the death struggle between the great military powers for control of Europe.

With brilliant perspicacity, Jewish leadership, with Chaim Weizmann at the head, recognized Israel's chance to realize its hopes in the event of a German defeat. With indefatigable zeal and careful strategy they watched for the opportune moment, and at a critical stage of the struggle, Great Britain, seeking support from every possible quarter, issued the now famous Balfour Declaration of November 2, 1917. It is of interest to note, however, that, according to Weizmann, both Lloyd George, who was then Prime Minister, and Lord Balfour himself, then Minister of Foreign Affairs, were greatly influenced in favor of the Balfour Declaration through religious and idealistic motives, while other members of the Cabinet were either indifferent or hostile.

[49]

To the Zionists, it was a great windfall and a needed shot in the arm. Even the rich and powerful Jews of Europe and America, who, at that time, still disdained Zionism, stood up and took notice. Zionism all of a sudden became a topic in the halls of international diplomacy. It happened at the right moment, too, for by that time the hope of Western Jews for the enlightenment and political progressiveness of European Christianity about the Jewish status had petered out, and disillusionment took its place. During that same period, anti-Semitism mushroomed in Europe. The Russian revolution was about to realize its goal. Besides, a goodly number of Russian Jews had migrated to the United States and other parts, and had lost direct interest in the Russian struggle. In short, world Jewry was ready for the Balfour Declaration.

But one of the arts of diplomacy is to say one thing and mean another, or at least to say it in such a way as to be susceptible to several interpretations. To the diplomat, the science of semantics is to pick words that can be twisted to mean whatever you want them to mean. In the instance of the Balfour Declaration, the wiles of diplomacy are illustrated. However, it must be admitted that on this issue both sides were cagy. Weizmann and the other Zionist leaders aimed for ultimate political sovereignty, or, at least, political autonomy in Palestine; but, being a minority in the ratio of about one to three among the Arabs, the precepts of democracy made such a demand inadmissable. They hoped that unrestricted immigration and land purchase would in time enable them to become a majority. This, with predominant land ownership, would also in time assure them the actuality of sovereignty. Hence, their successful effort to have the mandate to Great Britain from the League of Nations contain the right of unlimited immigration at least up to the point of absorptive capacity and unlimited land purchase—rights which England later repudiated. These circumstances, and neither oversight nor inaptitude in the choice of words or phrases, explain the equivocal language of the Balfour Declaration.

While Zionist hopes were thus raised, there came a kaleidoscopic change in the international picture. The most backward European nation, Russia, threw off its political shackles and appeared on the world horizon with a new order and a new dream. To understand how and why that affected Zionism, it is again necessary to turn back several pages of history.

[50]

CHAPTER IV

ENGLAND'S DOUBLE CROSS

For over a century Great Britain was the arbiter among nations, mistress of the seven seas, and the world's greatest military and commercial power. The sun never set on its empire. With all that, Great Britain was judicious, moderate, and hardly ever went to excess in the exercise of its power. Its motto was to live and let live. Its government, though a monarchy, was the most liberal on the continent, if not in the world, and its parliament a pattern for all other parliaments the world over. Great Britain was not given to sudden political outbursts and upheavals; its last revolution was in the days of Cromwell in 1649. Hence, it had time to dig in, become sturdy, stable, and dependable. True, it exploited other nations and peoples through its position as the leading industrial, commercial, colonial and banking power. But that, too, was in moderation. Anyway, in that exploitation, it followed certain definite, clear, international rules and customs, a contrast to the way of erstwhile Eastern tyrants. It likewise engaged in conquests of backward nations in Asia and Africa, and when, mistaken though it may have been, the need arose, England employed ruthless, cruel, and uncivilized methods to attain its ends. But once that was over, it re-established order, and was not wantonly vengeful or cruel. Often, the order established was a better one than the aborigines had known under their chiefs, when they had enjoyed so-called independence.

On the continent in Europe, Great Britain maintained its position and prestige through the theory of political balance. It saw to it that no one nation or group became too powerful. In that way, it became embroiled in a life and death struggle with Napoleon when he was riding high and all of Europe was at his feet. Great Britain was never eager for a fight, but when aroused fought doggedly and stubbornly. That's how this country earned the sobriquet of "John Bull." For over ten years, off and on, it fought Napoleon and was bled white, but in the end retrieved the balance in Europe, and in not too long a period also retrieved physical and financial strength. In fact, Great Britain became more powerful and more feared than ever.

Merrily, the island Empire went on playing the game on the chessboard of international politics, until it met the Teutonic fury in World War I. Once again, it was caught in the maelstrom to prevent the domination of Europe, and perhaps the world, by a combination of Germanic nations. This time the struggle did not last a decade, as did the Napoleonic Wars, but the concentrated effort during the four years it did last, was more costly in blood and treasure and more exhausting. Indeed, Great Britain came dangerously close to going down in defeat, together with the group of powers on whose side it fought, and was saved in the last hours of the war by the young Anglo-Saxon giant from across the Atlantic.

Still, with average luck and according to precedent, England, in a decade or two, was expected to emerge from this struggle, perhaps stronger and with more prestige than ever before. But here an entirely new and uncharted phenomenon appeared on the horizon. The Russian Revolution not only threatened world domination, but the whole fabric of the economic order on which England and its ruling classes had grown fat and powerful. It had just destroyed the German tiger and faced the Russian bear—not the old and sometimes friendly bear that could be appeased with a morsel or two, but an altogether new species that appeared to be set on growing fast. Old weapons and old tactics did not work, and the English lion was troubled and sorely puzzled.

In this situation, England decided to try an old trick, one that had so often succeeded and had brought such good results. Why not build up the prostrate German tiger, get him on his feet, and set him up to take care of this new and baffling bear? By this strategy, these two countries were expected to weaken each other, and at the proper moment the lion would step in and reassert its position as referee and ruler of the roost. Great Britain might even be lucky; Germany and Russia might mangle each other badly enough to require a taxidermist for their hides. That would indeed be a handsome addition to John Bull's historical museum. But, if the new bear was different from the old, the new German beast with the little mustache was even more unlike the old Junker type with the elongated mustache, named Wilhelm. The old Germany had more or less fixed habits and traditions, and with circumspection could be handled. The new was even more unpredictable and treacherous than the new type of bear. When the melée was on, instead of turning on the bear, the tiger turned against its master, the lion, with a fury that almost defeated its benefactor. Fortunately for the lion, the Nazi beast was indiscreet enough to turn around and attack the bear, too; at this the lion and the bear joined their strength in a ghastly life and death struggle with the ferocious beast. Again, the timely appearance of the young giant from across the Atlantic—the second time in a generation—brought victory. The Nazi beast was laid low. But victory was won at an appalling cost—chaos, confusion, destruction and suffering to humanity!

For England, it signified all that and more. To England it was the death knell of the role it had played for several centuries. Its manpower was dangerously reduced. What there was left of its human resources was greatly impaired and demoralized; its material wealth was consumed, and, overwhelmed by debt, its position as the world's leader in finance, industry, and commerce was wiped away. Everywhere, the prestige of Great Britain was destroyed.

On top of this, and largely because of the above facts, some of the sins of its youth came home to plague England. Its misrule and ruthless exploitation in the Far East bore fruit in rebellion and resistance. Likewise, its mismanagement of India brought disaster.

The immediate future was bleak and uncertain. In these circumstances, what could a nation do? Indeed, what does an individual do after a ruinous conflagration? There is but one thing to do, and that is to salvage from the fire whatever is worth salvaging. Similarly, there was just one thing left for Great Britain to do—salvage what it could of its Empire, for without Empire, it inevitably would sink to a second or third-rate power. With only its tight little island in Europe, it could hardly live; at least, that was the way England looked at its predicament. When it took stock of its Empire to determine how and what could be salvaged, it found that the Mediterranean was the one thing it had to control at all costs; for the Mediterranean is the pathway to nearly everything left to England and well worth salvaging. It is unfortunate that England is challenged in this direction by her erstwhile rival and late partner, the Russian bear, who has cast a lustful and malignant glance in the same direction. The Soviet

[53]

Union claims, too, that it must have an outlet on the same sea. In the winter it is completely frozen in and needs access to a warm-water port. Russia makes no secret of it and says bluntly that it means to get such an outlet sooner or later. Another compelling reason to hold on to the Mediterranean ports is the vast oil reserves located in these parts. Both England and the United States depleted themselves of their vast oil reserves and must find means to replenish them. Until the scientists find something better, oil is the life fluid of every nation.

But around this rich oil area which is likewise the path to Britain's Empire, lie some six or seven Arab Mohammedan tribes or nations, numbering about forty million backward human beings sunk in sloth, ignorance, and superstition. The only possible way to reach them or to deal with them is through their sheiks and muftis who claim, and in reality have, both legal title to and actual possession of these cherished oil reserves. Some way must be found to get the co-operation of the sheiks and muftis. England had foreseen that necessity and started a campaign for their friendship in the early Twenties, long before World War II was considered possible. A step in this campaign was either to initiate, or to look with benevolent complacency upon, the organization of these tribes or nations into some form of union of Arab nations. Obviously the means—the cement for such a union—was racial, religious, and nationalist propaganda.

Of course, all this ran smack against the Balfour Declaration and the terms of the mandate. "Well, what of it?" shrugged the Colonial Office. "Do not Empire interests come before Jewish interests? Yes, we made certain promises, but who could have foreseen the turn of events when these promises were made? It's too bad, but the realism of today must come ahead of any ethical obligation of yesterday." This was virtually admitted by General Smuts, who said, "There are times when ethical considerations must yield to expediency." (*The Challenging Years*, by Stephen Wise, page 301) Thus, the Colonial Office must have put pressure on the British cabinets of the Twenties. If these arguments had any validity, then, how much more cogent and compelling they must have appeared in the light of the events briefly outlined here. Does it or does it not explain why a Churchill out of office excoriates the Government for breaking its promises inherent in the Balfour Declaration, and yet does precisely the same thing when he becomes the chief of the same Government? Does it or does it not explain why the Socialist Attlee and other spokesmen of the Labour Party, during a political campaign, lambasted Churchill and his Cabinet for repudiating the solemn pledges to the Jews and took a solemn oath to right this wrong, but, when in power, double-padlocked the gates to Palestine against the wretched remnants of Hitler's victims?

But to crown this infamy, there is still another chapter that, for sheer stupidity, wickedness, and raw cynicism, exceeds anything in the annals of human experience. Unfortunately the United States was not only a partner to it, but may turn out to have been its initiator.

Even while the war was still on and the danger from the Nazis was still formidable, there was a taint of mutual distrust and suspicion between Russia on the one side, and Britain and the United States on the other, although Franklin Delano Roosevelt did a fine job to hold it down to a minimum. It cropped out in the discussions on the time and place to open up the second front. Actual friction, however, set in almost immediately with V-J Day. Both sides were to blame, though it seemed that the irascibility of the Russians was worse than either of the other sides. Franklin Delano Roosevelt was no longer there to pour oil on the troubled waters. With each problem that the termination of the war presented, the haggling increased in bitterness. Up to that time, most of the clashes seemed to be between Molotov, representing Russia, and Bevin the British, with Byrnes trying to act as mediator. Then came the 1946 Congressional elections in the United States, with a sharp turn to the right. In their jubilance, the reactionaries in the United States conceived the happy idea that the time had arrived to have it out with communism once and for all, on the Lincoln-sounding slogan that the world cannot exist half capitalist and half communist. It did not trouble them much that the head of the Administration was not of their party, and an erstwhile New Dealer. They had taken his measure and found that he would swing in the direction that he thought would promote his popularity and his chances of re-election. They were not mistaken.

Postwar conditions presented a brilliant opportunity for capitalism to prove its mettle and to show in what respect it is superior to the Russian brand of socialism. That would not have been so difficult in the present demoralized economy of Russia. After all, when you take away slogans and name-calling, what do the people of the world ask for? They are tired, desperate and hungry. They are now not concerned with ideologies. They want bread, a roof over their heads, some clothes in place of the rags to cover their bodies, and a chance to heal their wounds. That is what the Greeks, the Finns, the Poles, and other peoples in Europe and elsewhere asked for. If the United States and socialist Britain had taken the lead in seeing to it that the peasantry and working classes were given an opportunity, or the hope, for a decent living by apportioning land among them, taking over industries to be operated by labor, aiding in establishing order and early reconstruction, they would have taken the wind out of the Russian sails. It need not have been confiscation or Marxism either. Some method of compensation to owners, by giving them government bonds in the regular capitalist manner, could easily have been worked out. That still would have been much cheaper than civil war and chaos. After all, they were in competition with the greatest propaganda system in the world—the Russian. They were trying to sell their product, the profit system, against communism. One would expect they would dress up their product in a fine wrapper and prove its superiority. That is what any salesman would have done. Instead, what did they do? They took the old, rickety, rattling model, which they knew would not work, and tried to force it down the throats of friendly, expectant customers. Moreover, they bullied and threatened them. They did not come to the decadent, brutalized land aristocrat and industrial plutocrat—the corrupt, creaky civil regimes of Eastern Europe—and tell them to clear out and make room for enlightened and decent democracy. They did quite the opposite. They loudly and boisterously let it be known that they would prop up the old, rotten regimes with all the means at their command.

However, it must be admitted that the myopia that prevented capitalism from recognizing its opportunity after the conquest of the Nazis and Fascists, can in no way be compared to the malicious betrayal of democracy by the Kremlin.

If current civilization survives the mauling and torture of the cold and the potential hot war between communism and capitalism, the events of our times will be recorded as the most bizarre and malignant in all history. The performance of the clique of mad conspirators who seized power and parade as the Russian government are without doubt the most frightful menace to humanity. The errors and callousness of the leaders on our side, who aimed at conserving the status quo, pale into insignificance when set against the appalling atrocities of that gang of international fanatics. After their own lives, and the lives of the nations over whom they ruled, had been saved by the sacrifice of our youth and untold wealth, after we had, consciously, and with open eyes, risked our national existence to save them from the Nazi ogre, Hitler, whom they now imitate, one would expect that in sane human beings there would beat a pulse of gratitude, and for their own sake as well as for the sake of the rest of humanity, including their former allies, they would give the world a breathing spell. Instead, they lost no time setting in motion the most ingenious and diabolic propaganda system ever devised for the conquest of the world. The most devastating phase of that propaganda is the new technique they employ. With us, and the rest of the world, words have meanings to convey thoughts and attitudes. These they completely subverted. Such simple words as white and black, freedom and slavery, progress and reaction, rectitude, crime, and recognized scientific and historical facts conveyed definite ideas and were the international tools of man's mind. These are deliberately twisted and contorted by the Communists. Where, in the past, it was possible to embarrass and shame the tyranny of the czars by exposure and publicity, the present-day Communist by challenging the basic facts of life, as well as the meaning of everyday concepts, destroyed the common medium for conveying ideas. Now chaos and confusion fill the void. The deep significance of the biblical legend of the Tower of Babel, where the language and thoughts of its builders became confused, first becomes clear. The great tragedy is that there is no vehicle or substitute for common understanding. For this crime, history will never forgive them.

But you may ask: What has all this to do with our main theme of the Jews in relation to Israel? Why go off on a tangent? The answer, in the perspective of current international conditions, is crystal clear. Our lives and fate in Israel and the Diaspora are so bound up with the rest of the Western World that it becomes a matter of no less than survival. Everything must be done to prevent the inundation of communism, which takes advantage of chaos and confusion for its foothold.

The young state of Israel, under the enlightened and courageous administration of the Ben Gurion government, has done in the Near East what the Labour government of England has been doing for Europe to prevent the spread of communism. Like that government it has been a factor in building up the necessary resistance. An even more important factor is that the Near East, for the most part, has not as yet emerged from an era of feudalism. They still live in the dark ages. Israel is ideally equipped to serve as the beacon light in the emancipation of the suppressed and benighted people of the entire Near East from the yoke and tyranny of their present rulers. These rulers are fully aware of this danger to them, as is proven by their hostility toward Israel and refusal to negotiate peace treaties.

The world must soon realize that Israel is the advance agent of civilization in the entire Near East and will bring social, economic, and spiritual redemption to that part of the world.

CHAPTER V

FACING FACTS

In setting up "Medinas Israel," in the face of what seemed in-
surmountable obstacles, the Jews have achieved the most spectacular heroic epic in their long history. It was not only an un-
paralleled victory on the battlefiield against great odds—for the
enemy received aid and encouragement from England—but also a
great diplomatic triumph. Besides the scheming and manipula-
tions by England's Foreign Minister Bevin, the maneuvers of
some of the most powerful American oil interests had to be overcome. All this required great finesse and keen mental agility to
avoid becoming the pawn of either the Western or Eastern powers
and yet remain in their good graces. At this moment, efforts to
crown these victories are being made in peace negotiations with
Egypt and with other Arab neighbors. Unless a major error is
made, or an unforeseen disaster intervenes, some modus vivendi
should be arrived at between the Israeli Government and its erstwhile enemies, which will bring about peace, as well as co-operation for mutual progress and growth.

When peace negotiations are concluded, the problem posed
here in previous chapters will call for a solution, namely: What
should be the attitude of the Israeli Government toward the Jewish communities in the United States and in the Diaspora, and
what, in turn, should the attitude of these communities be toward
Israel? This question inevitably involves the vital issue of the
material and spiritual contribution they will make to one another. To get a clearer perspective on this multiple problem, this
writer has sought to give a close-up of political Zionism by review-
ing the principal events since its inception more than half a
century ago. Through this, relating those past events to the present situation, it should be easier to reach a sound position.

In order to see the facts in their true relationship, it will be
essential for the Jewish masses, and, above all, their leaders, to
sober up from the autointoxication they had encouraged, al-

though their encouragement may have been a big factor in arousing the superhuman efforts to win Palestine. The need now is for a logical, and clearly calculated course. It will be desirable to replace hosannas and high-sounding generalities with realistic, though at times unpalatable, facts.

For the Jewish State to be able to maintain itself, certainly for the first few decades, it will require the material support of Jews in the Diaspora, mostly those who are Americans. Hence, it is vital that their position should be sound and wholesome. They must dismiss the thought that because of Zionism, their status here, as well as that of Jews in other lands, is just temporary and ephemeral. The Americans of Jewish faith must become integrated into American life even more than ever before and not be diverted by hopes that they or their descendants will eventually become a part of the Jewish life in Israel. For, aside from the material or economic aspect, the international status of Israel will present difficult problems. The present maze of international complications in the Near East touches Israel at many angles. Then, too, you cannot shut your eyes to the fact that internal dissension that did so much to undermine and bring disaster to ancient Israel and Judea, is again raising its ugly head, even before Israel is completely organized. It may be a bitter pill for some of the zealots to swallow, but they must realize once and for all that Palestine, even in Biblical times, was not the objective of all Jews since only a small minority were there. Today, at best, even a smaller proportion can expect to find a place to settle there. Hence, it can never be a complete solution to the Jewish problem of the world. Moreover, a Jewish State today will have less importance and significance than such a State would have had half a century ago, when Herzl was living. At that time there was apparently more chivalry and gallantry in diplomacy and international relations. A nation, no matter how small or weak, enjoyed certain prerogatives, prestige, and immunities, much as the bigger nations did, although, in the final analysis and in certain situations, weakness and smallness was always fatal. Today, diplomacy is more crude and brutal, and the advantage of an internationally recognized status is not as potent as it was. But, conceding that even today there are still some clear and tangible advantages to a people in a recognized international status, it is a long way from being the pillar of strength of a few decades ago, when such relations operated on a group balance of power. Today, that balance is reduced to two huge hemispheric super-powers.

Then, why blink at the sober fact that organically and psychologically the Jews are now, by choice, a dispersed nation? They must forget such alibis as why they are that, or how they happened to become that way. The fact is that they are, and, throughout recorded history, they were a dispersed nation. Can anyone envisage all of them being corralled into one territory or state? No matter what the advantages or temptations, they are by nature a people on the move, and it looks as though it will take a long time before they become more settled in that respect.

Much of Zionist propaganda consists of emotional and poetic rhapsodizing about their spiritual and Messianic function—the role assigned to them through the historical incidence as the "People of the Book." This designation is probably due to the fact that traditionally they excelled in ethical and spiritual leadership. It is in fact their national genius to be in the front ranks of enlightenment and progress—their contribution toward a better and higher civilization.

But all this should not render them starry-eyed, unrealistic, and impractical. They must remember that the fundamental requirements for a better, cleaner, stronger generation are the earthly, material needs of the race—food, shelter, and a wholesome environment. Only on that foundation can they erect a finer civilization—a more decent, justice-loving, spiritual race. *"Ain kemach ain Torah"* (No bread, no learning) is a sound Talmudic maxim. Comb through the pages of history, and you will find that the statesman or ruler who had the wisdom and forethought to look after the physical comfort and well-being of his constituents had nothing to worry about from dissidents, clashing ideologies, subversive movements, or critical propaganda. Such rulers were able to perpetuate their rule and enjoy public esteem indefinitely, no matter whether the form of government was democracy, oligarchy, monarchy, or even dictatorship. That, in the final analysis, is the actual basis of communist strength, and the reason why communism has permeated the masses wherever it has been established. This is not intended as a satirical or cynical reflection on human nature. You cannot possibly expect a human being to develop the finer qualities, such as forthrightness, kindness, altruism, idealism and the other virtues, unless he is supplied with the elementary requirement for the growth of his body and mind;

[61]

he must also have the environment that will bring forth the flowering of the best that is in him.

That is why it is unrealistic to accept the over-emphasis by theology in general and Jewish theology in particular of the necessity of sublimating one's physical welfare to great spiritual levels. It is responsible for the asceticism advocated and prompted by so many demands of religious practice, such as fasting, lengthy prayers, long sedentary confinement in Talmudic research and casuistry, indulged in by the youth of the ghetto. Incidentally, some factions in Jewish life are now attempting to introduce this latter here in the United States. All this is presumed to be an essential preparation for some promised idyllic existence in some hazy hereafter, That, in ancient days, was the principal issue between Hellenism and Judaism, with the decision going to the Hellenistic point of view.

It should, therefore, be evident that the Jews must deepen their roots in the Diaspora and more than ever identify themselves with life around them. While Israel becomes established the Jews here in the United States must, in the first place, mend their political fences, so recklessly endangered during the many altercations over Zionism and Palestine. Their leaders have wisely or unwisely attacked many public men, from the President of the United States down, because of their attitude on issues arising out of the Palestine question. These, in one form or another, may come home to roost.

Finally, as their zealots sober up, they will have to realize that, at best, Israel, even after it becomes a model State with a high culture and territorial and numerical expansion, will never be much more than an important way-station in the destiny of World Jewry. It was never more than that in Biblical days. The fate of the vast majority of Jews will be, as of yore and despite present dreams, tied up and intermingled with the rest of the world. Time was when this world was considered vast, mysterious, and bewildering—when a despot, with a dozen towns, cities and large estates under his dominion, considered himself a king. If he happened to be cunning and daring, he collected a string of such kingdoms and declared himself an emperor. That day is gone. There is no longer room for that sort of game. The genie of science has set in motion a furious homogenizing process that will sooner than anyone now thinks possible crush the hard shell of nationalism and the other impedimenta—religious, political, or economic—that now keep nations and peoples in warring and mutually destructive camps. There is no longer room for small-ness—small business, small nations, small countries, and small thinking. Even now, though people are confused and bewildered by the tumult and threats, they see the subjugation of what only yesterday were "The Great Powers," and the emergence of two great giants that dwarf all others. These are communism and capitalism, glaring at each other and making frightful grimaces. But, sooner or later, this homogenizing force, after terrific noise and grinding, will compel the two to coalesce. When that comes about, we shall at last envisage the full flowering of civilization. We shall behold a new, modern monotheism, one universal reli-gion of justice and reason, one God speaking not through fanatics and self-appointed zealots, but, as He has always done, through His works and the laws of nature. Then, and not until then, will come to fruition the prophecy of Isaiah:

> *And they shall beat their swords into plowshares,*
> *And their spears into pruning-hooks;*
> *Nation shall not lift up sword against nation,*
> *Neither shall they learn war any more.*

ISAIAH 2:20, 4.

PART THREE

CHAPTER I

MEDIEVALISM IN THE 20TH CENTURY

1

In June, 1945, two hundred rabbis, constituting the Agudath Harabbanim (Union of Orthodox Rabbis), assembled in the Hotel McAlpin, New York City, and with all the ancient and solemn Hebraic ritual, excommunicated another rabbi, Dr. Mordecai M. Kaplan, on the charge that he compiled a prayer book which they, the orthodox rabbis, considered heretical. The ceremony included the burning of the books!

Upon reading the above item in one of our English language dailies, I rubbed my eyes to clear them and reread the item. I re-examined carefully the date line to make sure that it was not Amsterdam, Holland, 1633, when Uriel da Costa was put under the ban of excommunication, or 1656, when the same fate was meted out to Baruch Spinoza. But no; it did happen in the great metropolis of the freest Republic in the world in the middle of the twentieth century, only under much less provocation, and without the extenuating circumstances that led the Amsterdam Jewish community to act.

Ordinarily, such folly could have been laughed off as the irresponsible barbaric procedure of a benighted religious group; but, actually, it was symptomatic of a wave of frenzy that seems to have taken possession of the Jewish community throughout the length and breadth of the land. This anachronism is symbolic of the dissidence and confusion of the Jewish scene. On the one hand, there are reactionary clerics who seek to extinguish the light of reason and bring back medievalism, and on the other hand, a festering fascism which would employ force and violence for its ends and establish it as a State Policy. It undoubtedly expresses the dismay and desperation over the appalling ordeals of European Jewry during and after the Hitler reign of terror. That may explain the cause of the malady, but it offers no panacea.

What can be done to meet the threatened danger to Jews that such dissidence and incongruity is bound to bring? The solution may be found in reason and common counsel. Let us inquire, in the first instance, how the situation came about.

2

From the earliest period, organized religion—Jewish and Christian alike—as it gained power and prestige, sought rigidly to enforce fundamentalism and punish heresy or scepticism. It ruthlessly destroyed, whenever it had the power, anyone who made the slightest effort to humanize or rationalize religion with an expanding science. Though they had many triumphs, in the end they fought a losing battle against reason and enlightenment. They could not and did not stop the large number of deists who denied the existence of an anthropomorphic God—the God described in the Bible. With that went the belief in miracles, magic, and superstition, including beliefs in a holy trinity, immaculate conception, divinity of Jesus, the Messiah fable, and hundreds of others. It was a definite and clear measure of the growth and extension of enlightenment that such world celebrities as Spinoza, of the 17th century, Voltaire and powerful Frederick the Great, of the 18th century, and, in this country, Paine, Jefferson, Emerson, Thoreau, Ingersoll, and many others of the 19th century, dared to be deists.

This however, is most curious and puzzling. In the period since these great figures lived and rendered their invaluable services, the physical sciences made the most phenomenal strides, while the field of spiritual advance suffered the greatest setback. Today, a Christian could hardly get himself elected dog-catcher if he professed doubt in the divine origin of Jesus or the holy trinity. True, denominations will now tolerate deviations and fundamental differences in creed, but, insofar as the individual is concerned, he is expected to conform to all the tenets of his particular religion as they are promulgated by the church hierarchy. Everyone, at least in public life, is expected to adhere to one or another denomination. A so-called deist or agnostic would stand little chance of political success.

Change and evolution in nature, like everything else in nature, operates in orderly fashion and with predictable regularity. Thus, astronomers and physicists compute and predict phenomena, decades and centuries in advance. This is not so in human affairs. These work in fits and starts, sometimes called cycles. No schedule or system of their operations has yet been formulated. Hence, no statesman, sociologist, or historian can predict even for the briefest period the turn human events will take. Despite that, however, certain social, political, or economic happenings do yield to analysis and foreseeable reactions. In this way, it is possible to trace the cause of certain movements.

By this process, it is possible to place the present religious resurgence in its proper perspective. It is general and well-nigh universal. It manifests itself in the crusades for religious awakening, newer and more resplendent temples and synagogues, and the number of successful drives for funds and membership that bring greater wealth and power to religious bodies everywhere.

It also exerts considerable influence in other than the purely material sphere. Its influence on contempory literature is to be noted in the cycle of books such as Franz Werfel's *The Song of Bernadette,* Lloyd Douglas' *The Robe,* Bruce Marshall's *The World, the Flesh and Father Smith,* Sholem Asch's *The Nazarene, The Apostle, Mary,* and a number of others. How much these authors were influenced, if at all, by the prospect of gain, is irrelevant, because it does prove that there is a vogue and demand by the public for such books. Even such outstanding historians and thinkers as Arnold J. Toynbee, as shown in his *A Study of History,* and the more recent *Civilization on Trial,* is caught up in this trend, though it is only fair to state that his concept of religion may be on a higher plane than that of the general public or the conventional theologians. Add to this the latest phase of the Buchman movement "Moral Rearmament" (and less known similar activities), and the revived interest in the writings of Kierkegaard, and one gets a fairly clear picture of what is meant by religious resurgence.

To be sure, one can trace this trend to what Toynbee calls "Times of Trouble" or world crises, brought on by two world wars, the threat of an impending third war, and the terrible resultant dislocations. People in distress, like other creatures in the animal kingdom, become panicky and grasp at straws. That is the way they reacted to the bubonic plague which was fatal to a third of the population of Europe in 1348, to the appalling suffering and bloodshed during the Thirty Years' War and the Hundred Years' War, and to every other great catastrophe. But,

[69]

invariably, with the passing of the tide of fear and helplessness, there is a return of courage and confidence. However, until that happens, independent and strong minds, who attempt to resist or to rationalize these fears, will be misunderstood and will face the gamut of abuse.

The Jewish phase of the same reaction is accentuated, not only by religious fervor, but by the revival of mysticism and a rash of writings by Martin Buber, Franz Rosenzweig and scores of others. A recent English translation of the monumental work by Professor Gershon G. Scholem, titled *Major Trends in Jewish Mysticism* (Schocken Books, 1946), is a veritable library on the subject. The sprouting Hassidic movement in the United States is another proof. The change toward a more conservative point of view is also noticeable among the erstwhile Yiddish journalists of the liberal and radical school. They seem to lack their former zeal and vigor in their dialectic crusades to rid the world of superstition, ignorance, and occultism.

3

Unlike most other national religions, the structure of Jewish theology is made up of two distinctly different trends. For convenience, they shall be termed by their functional nature: Priests and Prophets. In its early parts, the Pentateuch itself formulates a blueprint of an administrative hierarchy. It is limited to Aaron and his descendants, who are termed "priests" and Levites. They constitute the ecclesiastic and governing body, with Moses at the head. Their jurisdiction extended to every phase and department of life. The authority was, as stated, the Five Books of Moses.

Centuries later, when Christianity appropriated the term "priests," the Jews of the Diaspora adopted the term "rabbis" in place of priests, who succeeded to the same powers and authority as Aaron and the Levites. Thus, they exercised not merely religious but also civil authority at least to the extent permitted by the governments they lived under; this, of course, varied with the place, period, and type of government. It was these rabbis, who, through the centuries of the Galut, compiled the Talmud. While portions of the Talmud are credited to some of the rabbis by name, most of it is apocalyptic.

The Prophets on the other hand, Israel's unique gift to the world, were self-appointed moral preachers. True, most of them claimed direct inspiration from God but this claim was for the purpose of lending prestige and weight to their utterances. They did not enjoy tenure of office and were not beholden to the kings, or the rich and powerful elements of the community. Hence, they spoke from their hearts—not merely for their day but for posterity. They seared the consciences of the tyrants, the wicked and the wrongdoers, and gave Israel the sublime moral leadership which through subsequent millenia gave them their greatest influence. Says Dr. Abram L. Sachar in his *A History of the Jews* (page 61): "Out of the mire of Hebrew political life, the prophets rose like strange exotic blossoms. Their work is as surely the contribution to civilization as Hellenic art is the Greek contribution, and imperial law and government the Roman." Yet Jewish life was molded and hardened not by the lofty precepts preached by the prophets, but by the narrow dogmas and paradoxes of the Talmud; the result was physical stagnation and moral frustration. Through the centuries, it ultimately created that blighting influence to the intellect that creed and fanaticism always bring with them. In the ghettos of eastern Europe it paraded under the name of orthodoxy.

The first substantially organized and real resistance it met from Jews in modern times was from the Maskillim in the middle of the nineteenth century and the movements of the Enlightenment throughout Europe in the same era. By far the greater number of immigrants to the United States were the Forty-eighters from Western Europe, principally Germany, and the Eighty-firsters from Eastern Europe, principally Russia. These were imbued with the ideals inculcated by the forces of the Enlightenment from the West and the Maskillim of Russia. There was, however, a considerable difference between these two streams of immigration. The Jewish reform movement in Germany practically extinguished orthodoxy, Jewish ritual, and exegesis and other facts of Jewish life. On the other hand, the larger flow of the Eighty-firsters, especially the intelligentsia, were political radicals and iconoclasts in matters of religion. They, of necessity, were products of political tyranny and economic backwardness in the Russian milieu. Not all of them, of course, were intellectuals, but they created a climate of opinion which molded the spirit and mood of the masses, who had been thirsting for enlightenment after centuries of ignorance, and social and political ostracism and degradation. Since most of the eastern Jewish immigrants

[71]

were poor, they identified themselves with the laboring classes, the proletariat. Thus, at the beginning of this century we see a clear and distinct polarial or opposite alignment in the American Jewish community. On one side were the older, more affluent and more Americanized German Jews, the Forty-eighters; on the other side were the more radical, iconoclastic proletariat type, the Eighty-firsters. But along with the Eighty-firsters was a segment trailing them, who made up the nucleus of the Orthodox Jewish community. They were disowned by their western brethren and the thing dearest to them, their religion, was repudiated by their own children and grandchildren. They felt that they were fighting a losing battle, and their position was indeed pathetic.

Under these circumstances, one would logically expect that the Orthodox Jews would affectionately turn to Zionism, then sponsored by the Chovevi Zion societies. But that was not the case. For one thing, the sponsors of these societies were the Maskillim, their erstwhile enemies. Similarly, when the Zionist movement came into being, the principal leaders were not religious, and some of them had been assimilationists, such as Moses Hess, Herzl, and Nordau. Above all, it was a rationalist and secularist movement based on realism; it did not conform with the Talmudic prescription for the coming of the Messiah and the rebirth of the Jewish people. That accounts not merely for the nonco-operative attitude of Orthodoxy, but for the downright hostility they at first displayed. However, the First World War intensified the Jewish problem, and the advent of the Balfour Declaration gave the Zionist movement a great spurt. Overnight it became a world movement. On one side, it broke through the contempt of the German Jews and, on the other side, the apathy of the Orthodox who, by this time, developed more modern and cultured leadership in such men as Rabbi Meyer Berlin and Rabbi Wolf Gold. They greatly strengthened the Mizrachi, who created a powerful organization for the dissemination of their religious principles and wove them into those of Zionism.

For a clearer understanding of the current situation in the Jewish scene, it is necessary to go back a couple of centuries to the inception of Hassidism and its effects. It started as a revivalist movement designed to afford the Jews a modicum of comfort and an escape from their distress and intolerable environment. It promoted and encouraged ecstasies in religious and ritualistic practices such as genuflections, dancing, and jumping, similar to the present-day Holy Rollers. Mentally, they indulged in fantastic mystic orgies. In the part of the ghetto where it flourished, it succeeded in diverting the minds of its followers from the strain and grind of daily problems, although at the expense of their mental equilibrium. A by-product was the racket it built up for its leaders, known as the *Gitte Yidden,* the claim to occultism and miracles. While it is no longer in vogue (though here and there are efforts to revive it) the net effect of Hassidism was to promote and advance dogma, superstition, and ignorance.

This influence, like the general influence of orthodoxy, at first hardly affected American Jewish life. The heterodoxy of the Eighty-firsters, and the climate of opinion created by them, precluded such influence. In point of fact, the antics of the *Gitte Yidden* served as material for satire and some ribald humor. However, two factors influenced the American Jewish community. The proletariat radicals, or at least a great number of them, evolved into capitalists and industrialists. The second was the catastrophic onslaught by the Nazis on European Jewry. The entire civilized world stood aghast, frozen with horror at this bestial exhibition of terror. The first reaction on World Jewry was to close rank and form a phalanx-like unity for common defense. All visions of international brotherhood were eclipsed by despair and frustration. A half century of faith and hope in progress and humanity was destroyed. It brough back the ghetto mentality with its clannishness, chauvinism, and a nostalgia for its customs, manners, and ritualism. Even our brave sophisticates of yesteryear, who could see salvation for the human race only in universal understanding and good will, turned panicky, and our brethren of the Reformed ranks are now also flirting with Orthodox trappings and customs. It is, therefore, neither strange nor surprising that organized Orthodoxy here and abroad takes full advantage of this religious renaissance. They are not satisfied merely to regain territory lost in the middle of the last century to the Maskillim and the Enlightenment, but aim for complete domination of the mind and conscience of Jewry. The general religious upsurge, the public mind, distraught over political and economic problems and difficulties, aid and complement their propaganda. As ever, during periods of strain and stress, the masses are susceptible to appeals for divine intervention and the appeasement of celestial powers.

This, of course, is as far as our Orthodox brethren can go in countries where personal freedom still prevails, especially where church and state remain separate. However, where they wield direct political power as they do, in part now, in Israel, they show themselves in true form. Like the Catholic hierarchy, they demand absolute and complete control of the mind and conscience of youth. Parents are responsible for the care of their children, but the shaping and molding of character are the sole prerogative of the Orthodox cabal. In this respect, they insist on a complete monopoly not to be shared even with dissident Jewish religious schools like the Reformed or the Constructionists. But that is not all. Given their way, they insist on the right to interfere with and curtail the civil rights of every denizen in Israel. Their first demand is for a rigid blue Sabbath. Riding on buses, attending movies and theaters, cooking, smoking, and sundry other such indulgences are prohibited. Violations are considered to be misdemeanors. Even now, without political control, there have been many instances where these zealots rioted, and burned and stoned streetcars operating in Jerusalem on the Sabbath. Moreover, they insist on an ecclesiastical juridical system with separate courts and complete jurisdiction of marriage and divorce—a monopoly not to be shared with the rabbis of dissident Jewish religious organizations. The implications of such powers are alarming. If one should happen to love a non-Jewish woman, he will not be given a marriage license. The dire consequences of such a practice can easily be imagined. A good illustration of how a monopoly of marriage and divorce works out in practice is reported in *The Reconstructionists* (March 18, 1949). A childless widow wished to remarry, but because her brother-in-law was too young to give her *halitzah* (release from his obligation to marry her) as required in Deuteronomy 25:5, she could not get a marriage license. Indeed it would be most difficult to predict how deep and tragic the effects on the lives of thousands might be, if left to the tender mercies of Orthodox rabbis in their attempts to interpret and apply some crude and primitive biblical laws.

These, remember, are the exactions and demands of the Orthodox, who are a mere twenty per cent of the voting population. They probably now, in the opinion of many, constitute one of the most disturbing factors and a great menace to the state of Israel. Hence, the incident reported at the beginning of this chapter is typical and not to be discounted as merely the whim of an

irresponsible and ill-advised group. Nor have the passage of time
and intervening events affected their adamant attitude. At their
recent convention, the Union of Orthodox Congregations stressed
the ban forbidding Orthodox Jews to attend Conservatice or Reform services.

CHAPTER II

INTELLECTUAL RETROGRESSION

1

There is a saying that Jewish life, in the United States at least, patterns itself according to its surroundings. In this respect, too, Jewish attitudes follow the non-Jewish. Fifty years ago, the great complaint throughout Jewry was that the dominant note in American Jewish life was heresy. It was sustained by the facts. Almost the entire younger generation became alienated from the synagogue. One of the first signs in the process of their Americanization was partial and often complete emancipation from ritual and religious practices. Many were the clashes on the Jewish scene between religionists and non-religionists, with the religionists definitely on the defensive.

It is pertinent to inquire into the causes that brought about this change. Whatever the trends were then or are now, that brought religious reaction to the non-Jewish world, they must have operated in a similar manner and to the same degree on the Jewish population. There were, however, additional and special factors in Jewish life that accentuated the effect. The first, undoubtedly, was the steady change in the economic status of the Jew from the proletariat to the bourgeoisie, from the lower working class to the middle class. A general conservative attitude usually follows such a shift in status. Religion is a concomitant. A second important factor was the increase of nationalism among Jews, through intensive propaganda by the Zionists. While a segment of the Zionists were of a radical tinge, this applied only to the economic aspects. Even that fringe became more chauvinistic and revived old religious customs and traditions through a chain of youth schools and clubs. In Zionism, old traditions and religious customs are so interwoven with the political ideal that one complements the other. However, the most potent and dramatic force that brought about the religious upsurge was unquestionably the catastrophe to World Jewry in World War II. That appalling holocaust, the most tragic in history, fully aroused the herd instinct. The dismal failure of the Christian world to intervene prior to the outbreak of the Second World War—when intervention might have been effective—intensified the utter despair World Jewry felt and gave them comfort in the sense of ghetto oneness. The natural concomitant was the revival of old celebrations of Jewish holidays, ritualism, the building of more and more synagogues, yeshivas, parochial schools, and the return to ghetto customs, such as the wearing of the skull cap and encouraging the revival of Hassidism with its miracle-performing rabbis, or *Gitte Yidden*. One observes things on the Jewish scene that one would scarcely have believed possible a decade ago, such as old bar mitzvah rituals with the "talis" and phylacteries, the buildings of Succoths, and parading with the Torah on public streets. One may soon look for the ghetto "shaytel" (peruke or wig), the "kapota" (gabardine or long frock), the beard, earlocks, and other ghetto relics to make their reappearance. That would, indeed, bring back medievalism. On a larger perspective, on the economic and social levels, this renaissance of the Jewish religion is reflected in a vociferous and bold chauvinism. It manifests itself in a rash of extravagant drives of all kinds for new Jewish institutions—some wise and necessary, but many, far too many, wastefully duplicating existing facilities. Their upkeep alone is bound to become an intolerable burden to coming generations, when funds may not be as plentiful as now. Another feature of many of these new modern palaces is their glamour and ostentation, ammunition for those who criticize the wealth of the Jews. Still another manifestation of the "new look" on the Jewish scene is the brazen intolerance of the ultra-nationalists toward anyone who dissents from even so much as some trivial detail of their fixed standards and claims, which become galvanized into a ritual or dictum. It is the old fanaticism and narrow intolerance back in the saddle again.

One might ask: What of it? If that will bring a solution to the age-old Jewish problem, then what is wrong in people doing what they believe in and what gives them comfort? That's exactly the rub. These new religious jingoistic opiates are bound to bring disillusionment as devastating and distressing as similar nostrums did to former generations in Europe and the Orient. It gives rise to dreams of grandeur about their place among the nations—an unrealistic concept of exalted ethical and intellectual leadership. Such an attitude is charged with dangerous potentialities and complications for the Jews on the international arena.

2

Lest I be misunderstood, I shall at this point pause for a personal explanation.

There is a prevalent error that all who oppose organized religion with its numerous cults, its ritualism and bias, are irreligious, irreverent, scoffers at all things sacred and solemn. Nothing is further from the truth. Take this writer's experiences and reactions. He was born into, and brought up in an orthodox Jewish family, where discipline was rigid. His early years were constricted and drab. It was a constant "don't do this" and "don't do that." It seemed that every natural impulse was sinful. The methods of enforcing these inhibitions at home and in cheder (school) were arbitrary and often cruel, so that even one with the timid characteristics of this writer when a child, bitterly resented the injustice. What was more natural than that he should throw off the yoke at the earliest opportunity and adopt a critical and cynical attitude toward religious dogma and the ritualism? More than likely this experience, in similar form, was duplicated by hundreds of thousands of the youth in the ghetto. This early phase of their lives impressed itself on their minds during their mental development and received as much thought as economic and social problems. Indeed, with this writer, they co-mingled with the intricate problem of living. It dawned on him early in life, that because religion and ethics dealt with the proper adjustments of the individual toward his fellow men, and his duties and obligations toward society, they were inseparable, and hence desirable. Toward this kind of religion there is an innate pull and yearning. But it is shocking what the professional religionist and the institutional church and synagogue did to dilute this fine and lofty feeling.

It is a singular fact that while the Jews were credited with the destruction of paganism and polytheism by proclaiming monotheism, then regarded as a revolutionary doctrine, they have done little, if anything since then, to keep its theology in step with scientific, social, economic, and political developments. At least, that is implicit in the doctrine that since the compilation and canonization of the Torah by the group of great rabbis headed by the Scribe Ezra, no mere mortal may add, alter, or in any way change a iota of these sacred writings. One may, at his own risk, make what comments he pleases orally or in script, but they can never carry the weight and authority of those embodied in the original sacred and canonized writings. In other words, the commands, ordinations, laws, and detailed directions for living became rigid and static for all time. It became inevitable that in the process of time and through mutations in history, many of these precepts and doctrines clashed with the facts of life and indisputable and proven scientific theories. In this dilemma, the rabbis resorted to sophistry and invented the art of casuistry to reconcile these contradictions, some of which dealt with practices in the material and business details of life. These attempts became known as "pilpul" and in many instances served as dispensations for the non-observance of some cardinal religious do's and don'ts. An early concession of this kind was the principle that civil law, or the law of the land, may override ecclesiastical law. In other words, God's mandates must be subordinated if and when they collide sharply with the edict of the King or his satellites, except when such edicts interfered with such fundamental tenets as circumcision or the observance of the Sabbath or Kashrut (dietary laws). *Dino de malchiso, dino* (The law of the kingdom is binding). (*Bovo Kama,* page 113.) But as to infractions of minor and less fundamental ordinances, because of serious obstacles in the path of their observance, the rabbis managed somehow to explain away the absolute necessity of conformance through resort to sophistry, which at times made black look white, and white look black. "The more progressive rabbis . . . refused to accept the verbal interpretations of the Biblical injunction." (Max Reichler in *What is the Talmud?,* page 30) Rabbi Gamaliel the second ruled that one witness in a divorce is sufficient, although the Bible required two; and Rabbi Hillel practically nullified the Biblical cancellation of debts during Sabbatical years because it worked against the welfare of the community (*ibid*). Thus casuistry among Jewish spiritual leaders became an art and not too infrequently a factor in spiritual deterioration. It also left an unfavorable impression on the entire mental development of the Jewish laity in their relations with practical life in and out of their communal surroundings.

Of the Old Testament, only the Pentateuch or the Five Books

of Moses are considered the direct personal word of God delivered through Moses on Mt. Sinai. Obviously, from the religious point of view, they are sacrosanct and beyond adding, modifying, or amending. But there did grow up a massive body of commentary and interpretation known as Ketuvim, which together with the Pentateuch and Prophets made up the Old Testament. All these writings, except those credited to the Prophets by name (many of whom are also legendary), are apocryphal, which lend them a degree of mysticism and sacredness. Most religious people are reluctant to question or criticize such writings.

Add to these the vast treatises and commentaries, written by rabbis and lay scholars of the pre- and post-exilic periods in Jewish history which in time became known as the Talmud, and one is lost in a vast theological sea. You can fish in that sea, and your net will bring forth the oddest assortment of ideas and formulas, out of which you can spin and weave any proposition and prove or disprove any theory. Even this irreverent critic, by no means a Talmudic scholar, found support throughout this book for his contention that reason should predominate over faith in the story of Rabbi Eliezer, who maintained that miracles do not prove themselves. Rabbi Joshua, participating in the argument, announced that reason is no longer hidden in the heavens; it has been granted on earth, and it is the task of human reason to comprehend and explain things. (*Talmud, Baba Mezia,* pages 59, 59a.)

The historian Isaac M. Jost speaks of the Talmud as "a great mine in which are imbedded all varieties of metals and ores. Here may be found all kinds of valuables, the finest gold and the rarest gems, as well as the merest dross." (Max Reichler: *What is the Talmud?,* page 5)

Maimonides spent a good part of his busy life in an endeavor to bring some order and synthesis into the Talmud and produced, among other writings, his *Moreh Nebochim (Guide to the Perplexed)* and *Commentary on the Mishna.* In these and other works he attempted to reconcile philosophic speculation on the nature of the soul and immortality, with the Mosaic faith. In doing this, he explained away dogma and such fundamental beliefs as the resurrection of the dead, even as Philo did many centuries before him. For his labors Orthodox Jewry abused him and branded him a heretic and renegade. His writings engendered dialectical polemics almost down to our own era.

Thus, the efforts of good old father Abraham to rescue the ancients from a morass of many gods and the confusion of their conflicting interests and exactions, by giving the world one powerful Deity, universal and cosmic in stature, was dismally defeated. For so entrenched are the theological barnacles that encrust monotheism that a proper and intelligent understanding of the God idea is more difficult now than in the days of Abraham.

Next to the Catholics and perhaps Episcopalians, the Orthodox Jews tenaciously adhered to ritualism, and so failed to broaden and expand, to keep pace with the growth and development of the human intellect. Instead of casting aside the swaddling clothes of superstition, religion was wrapped in the dark era of its birth and was not permitted to take on forms that would enable it to attain vigor and intelligent growth. Instead, it became dry dogma and static formalism. Its exponents keep on proclaiming that its heart and soul is its ethics, epitomized by Hillel in the slogan: "Do unto others as you would that others do unto you." As an ethic, it should stand for living, for action, and for change and progress. But what does one see in actual practice? In the Orthodox Synagogue, the Ark, holy of holies, contains several scrolls in plush coverings, emblazoned with silver handles and gaudy tinsels. Then comes the talis (prayer shawl), the phylacteries, and recently in the ghetto, the beard, earlocks, and the gabardine were a "must" for every good Jew in Eastern Europe. Superimposed over and above these tangible manifestations was a body of ritual, designated "Taryag Mitzvos" (613 Ordinances) that touch on and constrict every human impulse. No Jew, past or present, could ever hope to comply in thought or deed with the multifarious requirements and inhibitions contained in the Torah and the Talmud. In a word, Orthodoxy is static, and a challenge to the natural law of growth and change. Since the modern person of reason regards all natural phenomena as a symbol of Deity, the work of the Creator, we confront the paradox of a medieval school of thought contradicting the very nature of God.

CHAPTER III

ORTHODOX, CONSERVATIVE, REFORM

1

I have thus far attempted a brief and perhaps sketchy review of
the practice and doctrines of the Jewish religion. I shall now offer
an equally sketchy perspective of the current inner content and
meaning of Judaism in the United States. Conforming Jews are
now represented by three principal institutions: Orthodox, Conservative, and Reform. Let us examine briefly their respective
tenets, claims and forms.

To the Orthodox, Judaism is a divinely revealed faith from a
personal God, the Creator of all animate and inanimate things
in the universe, and the arbiter of their fate. He deliberately
picked the Jew from among the entire human race as His spokes-
man. For this reason, He established contact and held communion
with their early ancestors, the three patriarchs, Abraham, Isaac
and Jacob, who from time to time received instructions, interdictions and promises; but He revealed His complete scheme or
law for the guidance of humanity through Moses by means of
the Ten Commandments and the Torah, which is known as the
Pentateuch, or Five Books of Moses, the Prophets and Scriptures.
The Oral Laws (Talmud), which superimpose the Torah, while
not of the same degree of sacredness, are also divinely, though
more indirectly, revealed. Both, however, are unalterable and not
to be questioned in any manner. They are sacrosanct. Orthodox
Jews, with admirable consistence, believe implicitly in all the
miracles related in the Bible and Oral Laws. Salvation, they believe, will come through the Messiah, who will bring peace and
brotherhood to the world. His coming, they predict, will also be
an act by the Grace of God, though some now condescend to believe that Zionism could be the agency chosen by God. The practice of his religion by the Orthodox Jew consists of extensive
daily prayers, observance of both the written and oral laws as

laid down by the Torah and the Talmud, including all ritual
and practices prescribed therein, in strict accordance with the
letter and the spirit.

2

At first glance, the Conservative Jews are a compromise between the Orthodox and Reform, but that is only so to a degree.
They share with both the belief in a personal God, and have
adopted some physical synagogue changes, which make them appear more progressive than the Orthodox. But actually they
adhere to most of the dogmas. They hold that the Torah is a
divine revelation and was handed down by Moses from Mount
Sinai. It follows that to them, too, the Bible is changeless, immutable, and sacrosanct, and must be accepted in the literal
sense, in the same way the Orthodox accept it. Yet, they say that
they do not use the term "Revelation" in its supernatural sense,
but "in the sense of deep spiritual insight and . . . that revelation
is progressive and therefore has changed in the past and must
constantly be adjusted to meet the needs of every generation."
(Dr. Bernard Harrison, Director Hillel Foundation, University
of California, in *Annals,* March, 1948). The meaning of this state-
ment is anybody's guess. How can "Revelation" be adjusted to
meet the needs of every generation? Like the Reform Jews, they
reject the traditional Jewish concept of the Messiah, who is referred to in their prayerbooks only as a "matchless symbol." (*Sabbath and Festival Prayer Book,* page 385). On the other hand,
"With regard to such concepts as prayer, sin, and immortality,
Conservative Judaism shares with Reform the modernist approach." (Rabbi Harrison, *Annals,* March, 1948, page 31). From
the above and similar pronouncements, as well as in the sermons
of Conservative rabbis, it is easy to recognize a trend toward expediency and opportunism. The obvious aim is to attract the more
progressive in the Jewish ranks with a brand of religion com-
pounded of seventy-five percent Orthodoxy and the rest Reform.
In this, they employ much double-talk with a jumble of cloudy
phrases, like a jigsaw puzzle, and one must be adept at putting
them together in order to get some form and meaning out of
them.

Conservative Judaism, which now probably attracts the bulk
of Jewry in the United States, is still in its formative and trial

and error stage, swinging from right to left and from left to right. However, one of its factions mostly concentrated in the New York area is potentially the most dynamic and challenging movements in Jewish Theology. It is Reconstructionism. It was founded in 1922 by Dr. Mordecai M. Kaplan, the target in the episode related in the beginning of the third part of this book. In a most disarming and alluring, even if somewhat disingenuous introduction, it throws open the doors of the synagogue to the most discriminating rationalist. If it were to carry its formulations and program to a logical conclusion, the pantheist, agnostic, rationalist, and philosopher interested principally in the ethical and spiritual aspect of religion could join and co-operate without stultifying himself. Ponder over these quotations, and draw your own conclusions:

> We Jews then, must try to discover why so many of us do not wish to be Jews, why some of us no longer find any spiritual inspiration in the Jewish religion. We must try to determine why many Jews seek to escape, why they are dissatisfied, unhappy, restless, ridden by doubts, by feelings of inferiority, by self-hate.

> We of the Jewish Reconstructionist movement are trying to face these problems boldly and frankly. Tho we are fully aware of the stampede from Jewish life on the part of large numbers, we believe that this flight can be stopped. We know that there are many Jews who desire to continue to share their common past, to assume mutual responsibility in the present and to work together for the best kind of future for the entire Jewish people. . . .

> There is still another unprecedented condition which has revolutionized Jewish life. In the Western world the impact of modern science and modern thought, has weakened and in many cases destroyed, the belief in the supernatural origin of religion. This trend affected the Jewish religion as well. Many Jews began to find it impossible to believe in the divine authority of Jewish Law and in the literal interpretation of the miracles recorded in the Bible. Thus we may say that the incorporation of the Jews into Western nations, together with the growing skeptical attitude toward revealed religion, has shaken modern Jewish life to its foundations.

> In this new era we should continue to emphasize that men can and must obey the law of God, *but the law should not be regarded as being confined to any one book or any set of books*. It can be discovered in everything that makes for a happier and better world. Jewish life should be reconstructed along democratic lines. Unity should be based on voluntary cooperation for common interest and purposes, rather than on an enforced conformity with traditional laws, customs and rites assumed to possess supernatural sanction. All matters which affect the Jewish people as a whole must be decided by the

community as a whole, by majority rule, after previous free and unfettered discussion. But all matters which do not require collective action by the community, such as the expression and practice of religion, must be treated in a way that permits full freedom of conscience without the application of any social pressure for conformity.

. . . We must view religion not as a supernatural creed or code of laws, but as the affirmation of the worthwhileness of life; as the search for a sincere faith through which to activate the desire to make the most of one's life. . . .

Introduction to Reconstructionism.

But it becomes very puzzling when the same authority who enunciated and expounded the foregoing enlightened and profound precepts says that among the many things expected of the Reconstructionist are: "Observe the ceremonies . . . Sabbath, Festivals, Kashrut and Prayer." Suppose that in the exercise of his rights and privileges, clearly contemplated by the broad and liberal precepts above quoted, an individual Jew or an entire Congregation decides to repudiate Kashrut, for example, or the observance of the ceremonies, or he repudiates prayer: Does he thereby cease to be a Jew? Is he, or are they, subject to expulsion as a Reconstructionist?

3

Reform Judaism, as the term implies, is a concept more in harmony with modern thinking. According to Rabbi Harrison, quoted above, "Reform Judaism meets the challenge of a modern world with the doctrine of progressive Revelation as the touchstone of its world outlook . . . it equates the term (Revelation) with the intellectual and moral evolution of mankind . . . it posits a system of rational beliefs and arrives at a universal faith which is the essence of Judaism . . . hence the idea of God has been subject to a continuous development in Jewish thought" (*Annals,* March, 1948, page 28).

If this definition of Reform Judaism is somewhat abstract and lacks clarity, it at least conveys the idea of resiliency, modernism, and rationalization in the concept of deity as compared to the dogmatism and immutability of the Orthodox doctrine.

A discussion of present-day Reform Judaism in the United States is more complicated than a discussion of either Orthodox or Conservative Judaism. Towards the latter half of the 18th century the philosopher Moses Mendelssohn paved the way to bring modern culture to the Jewish scene in Germany. A group of eminent intellectuals carried on the movement and popularized it. Finally, hardheaded businessmen translated it into action by starting Reformism. It is to be noted that in the beginning they had no rabbinate of their own; the current rabbis fought them as hard as they dared. The theologians of the day who may have been in sympathy with the movement were not, at first, sticking their necks out. Not until the Reform Movement started to take root and showed unmistakable signs of success did they begin to flock to its banner. In short, Reform Judaism was not initiated by a Martin Luther.

However, it grew rapidly and attracted to its fold some of the able theologians, who soon gave shape and tone to its ecclesiastical content. This situation created a unique opportunity in Jewish history, with tremendous potentialities. Reform Judaism, as stated, was at first a bold and frankly utilitarian civic enterprise among the lay community. The intellectual and middle class Jews in Germany wanted to get closer to their generation of non-Jews and, as far as possible, bridge the ideological gap between them. Breaking down the walls of ghetto medievalism appeared to them a good start. Right or wrong, that was their approach to the change. But the rabbinate had the unusual chance of taking the long view of its opportunities by bringing Jewish theology up to date, first, by cleansing it of its superstition and occultism, and second, by bringing it into harmony with science and the humanities. In this way it would have re-established its universal religious leadership. In this, it failed. To show how and why it failed, it is necessary to retrace in some detail certain aspects of Jewish theology and Jewish philosophy.

The ancient Greeks were, without a doubt, the progenitors and pioneers of early philosophy and undisputed masters in that field, even as the Hebrews were in the field of theology. In developing their sciences, the Greeks used sense perception through the method of observation and inference, induction, and deduction. Their implements and equipment were the five physical senses. In the main they kept their gods and religion separated. This was not so with the ancient Hebrews, who first came in contact with Greek philosophy in Alexandria in the pre-Christian era. Being influenced by and attached to these two diverse and conflicting cultures, the Hebraic and Hellenic, they felt the need

[86]

of a synthesis and harmonization of both. Thus was born the Judeo-Alexandrian School of Philosophy. Its effect, however, was baneful and unfortunate, as any attempt to ride two conflicting hobbies was bound to be. The Hebraic and Hellenic elements never did mix; they only brought about a schizophrenic monstrosity, which was neither philosophy, nor metaphysics, nor revelation. It was responsible for much confusion and precipitated internecine struggles and bloodshed among Jews.

The trouble was that early Jewish thinkers and leaders toyed with the idea that they could tie the two together by some high-sounding sophistry. Greek philosophy, they said, is based on reason, starting with mind and matter. But does not mind, reason, and matter emanate from God? Is not God the Source of (1) Intellect, (2) the universal Soul, (3) Nature and (4) Matter? In this mixture you have the Neo-Platonist School, an artificial concoction of Greek Philosophy and Hebrew Revelation. To this was added a pinch of what might be termed "divine reason and ethics." The argument ran like this: Is it fair to assume, much less insist, that "Divine Revelation," the Hebraic element in this new philosophy, should be restricted to and limited by the mere physical rules of reason or human pragmatism, or just ordinary common sense? Surely, they argued, the ordinary five physical senses are inadequate to define or equate. Nor, they contended, could one be enthralled by these higher "Divine Revelations." "It takes," they said, "great spiritual perception, a sublime exaltation, to penetrate a transcendant intellect, which is in fact God. True, ordinary mortals can scarcely aspire to such exaltation, but in rare instances an exceptional individual reaches a state of ecstasy, enthusiasm, and transfiguration, in which, losing consciousness of himself as an individual, he may momentarily enter into a mystic union with the source of all being, God." Here, then, is the pattern of how the portals of philosophy, or so-called philosophy, were opened up to occultism and supernaturalism. How the lively, imaginative, and poetic Jewish brain loved to revel in fantastic, metaphysical speculation on the divine nature and attributes of God! Several notable historical Jewish figures, including Philo, and, later, Maimonides, Ibn Daud, Gersonides, and Crescas, employed this thesis as the cornerstone of their systems to identify God with Nature. Their speculations were a step in the direction of intellectualism, inasmuch as they broke away from the static concept of Godhood. Moreover, these

[87]

speculations were esoteric, limited to the upper level, and did not percolate down to the masses. The tragedy came later, when sinister frauds or even some honest fanatics made use of this school of thought as the foundation of mystic symbolism and gained much power and influence among the masses. If, on a philosophic and rational basis, it is possible to establish communion with God, then how can you check the claims of any charlatan or quack from setting himself up as an emissary of Deity? That's exactly what happened. Wading into the vast epistology of the Christian Mystics, the Cabala, and other parts of the Talmud, charlatanism and superstition went on a rampage. Hundreds, if not thousands, of pretenders and frauds organized new sects and spread confusion and disunity. They built roadblocks in the path of clear thinking and promoted conflict and bloodshed. For nearly fifteen hundred years, they kept the human mind in a tumult of ignorance and bitterness. Hassidism among Jews is just one of its wild flowers. Much of the separatism and the ardor of the Ashkenazic attitude, as interpreted by Professor Heschel, is based on the same false hypothesis.

When the rabbis of the German and American Reform Judaism came on the scene, they not only adopted the physical changes begun by the lay founders and revised the liturgy to conform to these changes, but they went a step further. They reached out for the "soul" and spirit by boldly challenging the authority of the Talmud. They said in effect: Surely, we will study it like any other exegesis in our theological curricula, and extract from it any pearls of wisdom we can find, but we will no longer permit it to mar our daily existence with endless encroachments and restrictions. In this manner, they freed themselves and their followers from what came to be recognized as an intolerable burden, one that even those who had not formally repudiated the authority of the Talmud had repudiated through neglect.

Had they shown the same commendable courage with respect to the Pentateuch and the other books in the Old Testament, by clearly and boldly announcing that they evaluated the Old Testament as a wonderful collection of great works containing precious literary gems—a fine ethical and spiritual code to be perused and studied but not worshipped—they would have laid the cornerstone of a universal religion, one that would fit the times and mood of this generation. Instead, they set up a paradox. They took a clear and unequivocal position when they rejected the doctrine of canonization of the Torah she-ba-pay (Oral Law) and rejected the binding doctrine of the Talmud, but lost their nerve to do the same with the Torah she-bi-csav (Holy Writ) represented by the Old Testament. That they accepted uncritically as the "word of God," but not in the simple literal sense as the fundamentalists do. Since throughout the Old Testament God is unmistakenly endowed with personality and human traits and is deeply involved in the affairs of each human being, as well as in the myriad other things that keep on happening, the Reform rabbis dipped extensively into the Neo-Platonist school of philosophy to explain and interpret God. In doing so, they were actually imitating Philo and Maimonides. This resulted, as it was bound to, in such a morass of equivocation, that it enabled one to make of God what he will. To put it another way, instead of man being made in the image of God, God is the product of the image of man. By way of illustration, here is an excerpt from *The Jewish Idea of God*, by Samuel S. Cohon, published under the imprimatur of the Central Conference of American Rabbis; his approach to the problem is both reasonable and modest:

What God is in His infinity and majesty beggars the mental capacities of mortal man. It has been well said that to comprehend Him fully the human mind must have to excel Him. We have to content ourselves with feeble guesses regarding Him. In this essay we set for ourselves the still humbler task of sketching, in brief outline, the answer to the question: What meaning has Judaism attached to the idea of God?

Though the belief in the ever living God always has been central in Judaism, it was not always conceived in the same way. Like every other product of human experience, so the idea of God has been subject to continuous development. In response to the growing needs of men and with the advancement of knowledge and of moral refinement, certain notions once held regarding the Divine were later found unworthy of Him who represents the highest perfection, and were replaced by more suitable ideas.

But note how subtly he files a notice of proprietary claim to occult perspicacity for the rabbis, in the following paragraph:

The consciousness of the holy, which discloses new levels of truth and of value to man, assumed its richest forms in the vision of the prophets. As nature yields her secrets to scientific minds and its beauty to poetic and artistic genius, Divine truth communicates itself with special fullness to prophetic spirits, attuned to perceive its overtones. The process of revelation is progressive and universal, confined to no one age and to no one people. Men of religious genius of all times and of all races have been vouchsafed glimpses of His truth. In ancient Israel, it may be said to have reached its highest level. The prophets were irradiated by the Divine, and became the clearest seers of His truth. The voice of God resounded within their conscience, calling man to loyalty and to obedience as conditions of true living.

Then he gently chides science for going beyond its depth, thus:

From our brief historical survey of the God idea in Judaism, let us turn to its permanent elements. The Alpha and the Omega of Judaism is the reality of God. Like all truths, so this one has not gone unchallenged by the opponents of religion. As in the past, so today, the challenge comes principally from the realm of natural science. In the thousands of years that have passed since Judaism arrived at the monotheistic world-view, science has made remarkable progress. It has unveiled a limitless universe, of vast spaces and unending time, of myriads of stars and of planets of gigantic dimensions. We are baffled by the immensities, the marvels, and the potentialities of the bewildering pageant of the skies. Extending the reign of law to all departments of existence, science clashed with the belief in miracles, i.e., of the occasional intervention of God in the processes of nature for the benefit of man. Under the spell of triumphant reason, which has established the interconnection of the natural order and the unbroken continuity of the evolutionary process, the whole idea of God appeared to some thinkers as a useless hypothesis. The universe, they maintain, can be accounted for without Him. To unify and to organize our multifarious experience of the outside world and to understand the scene of our life, they revived the ancient philosophy of materialism, which rests on the assumption that the universe constitutes a sort of vast machine. It is an aggregate of physical forces which operate with undeviating regularity. However complex it may appear, nature in all its parts reduces itself to mere matter and force. Even such things as consciousness and conscience, mind, will and personality are but products of matter.

Picturing the world as a colossal automatic engine seems congenial to the thinking of men in an age that has witnessed the greatest triumphs of the machine. To numerous minds it recommends itself as a common sense view which does away with much of the fog that has enveloped reality. The difficulty with this picture is its over-simplicity. While there is a mechanistic aspect to nature, mechanism fails to account for its inmost character. The symbol of the machine does not represent adequately the tiniest living organism, let alone the wondrous universe in which we live. The mysteries of generation and of growth, of consciousness, of intelligence and of distinction between right and wrong, etc., hardly belong to a machine. Those who think of the universe in terms of mechanism overlook the further fact that no machine is self-made. Our engines, even if they be automatic, are the products of the

human mind that designed them. They did not originate themselves. The loco-
motive, the automobile, the watch—they are all manifestations of the mind
that invented and designed them. Consequently, the measure of the machine
for the universe fails to carry out the real intention of the materialists. It does
not wholly do away with creative thought. Though we may recognize the mechanistic aspect of nature, we are not compelled to abandon its spiritual
aspect. An adequate picture, under which we may view the world, must re-
flect not only the material or quantitative side of reality but also its spiritual
or qualitative side, its order and beauty as well as its size and power. It must
include not only inorganic matter, but also its capacity to produce organisms,
consciousness, and intelligence.

Finally, he winds up with a more somber admonition to science that it stay in its own yard of applied science and not meddle
in the metaphysical—the exclusive preserve of theology. This is
entirely in keeping with its universal age-old loud and vigorous
warning to "keep off" on all metaphysical and ethical questions,
which it claims as its exclusive monopoly. Religion is its stock in
trade, and woe to anyone who challenges that claim. From its
very inception, theology shook a warning finger. One of the first
incidents in Genesis is the Adam-and-Eve apple episode. Because
Eve yielded to temptation and ate the apple of the Tree of
Knowledge, all posterity was doomed. Later, a group of innocents
became a little too curious about the workings of "heaven" and
started building a tower to get up there (Tower of Babel) to find
out for themselves. For their curiosity they were punished by
having their language broken up into many dialects with utter
confusion resulting. These episodes indubitably point to the
moral that mere *homo sapiens* had better leave "heaven" and all
curiosity about celestial things alone, for that is the exclusive and
private concern of the priests and professors of religion. That is
the clear implication of these legends. There is further proof of
this in the fact that during the Middle Ages the clergy made it
a capital offense to translate the Bible from the Latin into the
vernacular.

The charge that science is mechanizing and materializing religion and thereby blaspheming God is a brazen falsehood. It is the
men of science who, by their studies and research, have given us
a glimpse into the majestic stature and infinite sublimeness of
God. It is they who are tireless in their incessant endeavors to
discover and learn His laws and the secrets of the cosmos, which
they freely and proudly pass on to all of us. They thus give

dignity to the power and greatness of the Creator. For their in-defatigable labors and unselfish devotion to an ideal, they were persecuted and burned at the stake. Now when they can no longer make martyrs of them, the clergy cringingly plead with the men of science to leave their "heaven" alone.

What do these men of religion offer us in lieu of the fascinat-ing theories and inspiring truths about God's profound secrets in the immutable and mostly predictable laws of nature which the scientists have unearthed and promulgated for us? They sub-stitute a bewildering collection of apocryphal and anonymous legends, folklore and other writings under the title of the "Old Testament" and "New Testament." Some of these collections are canonized into Holy Writ. They claim that a physical being they call God abased himself by coming down from his celestial abode to hand them over to poor, evil-disposed human beings through a favored messenger. Don't dare ask for their proofs! You are consigned to perdition if you harbor any doubt or question the thousand and one confusing and conflicting dogmas contained in these two "Testaments." The clergy alone has ir-revocable license to speak for and interpret God's laws and His will. To hold on to this privilege, they built up the vast inter-national empire called Organized Religion. Theology has en-trenched itself by inspiring in the masses an ambivalent fear and love complex for religion, and a hate complex for dissidents. Some of their tools are ritual, ceremonials, and prayers. That the leaders of Reform are aware of this lack of consistency and vacuity in their concept of God, is clear from the proceedings of the mid-year conference of the Institute of Reform Jewish Theol-ogy, held at the Hebrew Union College in Cincinnati in March, 1950. The principal questions posed at that conference were: "Is the belief in God as an objective divine reality indispensable to modern Judaism, or must it be replaced by something more agreeable to the modern temper?" . . . "Is it possible for man to believe that an existing God is active in our world?" Though the expectation that these questions would be taken up for discussion brought a large attendance to the conference, and the questions were actually argued and discussed for over two days, no clear and satisfactory answer was formulated. They had to content themselves with the adoption of a five-point program defining and strengthening the mission of the Reform movement. (For a more complete report of the Conference see: *Commentary*, June, 1950, page 567.)

CHAPTER IV

THE MODERN JEW

What should be the attitude of the modern, nonconforming, independent-thinking Jew who belongs to none of the three organized schools of religious thought here set forth? Of course, the Orthodox creed denies him the right to any doubts or deviation from standard and regularized practices, even though God endowed him with the factulty to think for himself. "To change the Torah of Moses, we need a Moses." (J. H. Lookstein, *Orthodox Judaism,* Discussion Group, Anti-Defamation League, Chicago, Pamphlet #30, page 7). But how is an individual, or an entire community, to recognize a new Moses? As a rule, many such men, destined for immortality, are never recognized in their lifetime. Many referred to Moses Maimonides as another Moses, but he was anathema to the Orthodox group, to many of whom he is "traif" to this day.

The more elastic and reasonable position of the Reform movement opens the door to such discussion. Moreover, the best modern thought urges a broad analysis and discussion of religion. Thus, Erwin R. Goodenough (a non-Jew), professor of the history of religion at Yale University, and author of a number of scholarly works on Jewish theological subjects, says, in his article titled "Needed: Scientific Study of Religion" (*Commentary,* March, 1948, page 275): "There is only one course left for those of us who do not want to relapse into traditionalism . . . we must begin a study of religion and ethics in which we use not less, but more scientific method. What needs to be tried is a real attempt, for the first time in history, to be scientific in the study of religion. By scientific, I mean that we gather data not to prove that Jesus, Hosea, Mohammed or Karl Marx is right or wrong, but in order to find out what the religious experience of man has come from, where he gets his ideals, and which ideals have worked constructively and which have not."

In the same vein, Elliot E. Cohen, editor of *Commentary* (May,

1948, page 412): "By and large, what we have to offer in religion and culture does not begin to satisfy thoughtful Jews of American birth and background. They are critical or, worse, totally oblivious. The ranks of the 'unaffiliated' represent a large majority of all American Jews and these ranks are growing."

The rational and moderately conservative Will Durant, though not a Jew, makes this contribution to the question: "If there is any intelligence guiding the universe, philosophy wishes to know and understand it and reverently work with it; if there is none, philosophy wishes to know that also, and face it without fear." (*Mansions of Philosophy*, page 21.)

If, then, there is any merit in this modern trend of thought, the objective free mind asks in the first place, "What is God?" Is He physical, corporeal, a personal god in human form, such as the Jewish and most other theological schools teach; or is it the great, inexplicable, unrevealed, cosmic force that rules and guides the forces of nature? Let us consult some of the great minds on the question.

Aristotle said: "God is a being incorporeal, invisible, spaceless, sexless, passionless, changeless, perfect and eternal. . . . He is the final cause of nature, the drive and purpose of things, the form of the world; the principle of its life, the sum of its vital processes and powers, the inherent goal of its growth."

Spinoza's view on this was: "God is the imminent and not the extraneous cause of all things. All is in God—all lives and moves in God. God and Nature are one and the same."

Hegel defines God as the "absolute, and the absolute is the sum total of all things in their development. God is reason, and reason is that web and structure of natural law within which Life or Spirit moves and grows. God is Spirit and Spirit is Life."

An oriental view equates God with Truth, as in the following: "Truth is the law of God. . . . Truth means the realization of our being. Truth is that by which things outside of us have existence. This absolute Truth is indestructible. Being indestructible, it is eternal. Being eternal, it is self-existent. Being self-existent, it is infinite. It is transcendental without being conscious. Because it is infinite and eternal, it fills all existence."

In terms of the above formulations, the choice for the modern is either the anthropomorphic Deity proclaimed by each of the three branches or schools of thought in Judaism, or the pantheistic philosophy of the Ancient Greeks, of Spinoza, Voltaire— deists of the type of Emerson, Paine, and Thoreau, together with a great number of the best minds of the past and present. The question can be asked: Why is it that the personal God of the Jews and many of the other institutional creeds to whom the followers attribute the exercise of the human functions of thought and speech, has not revealed Himself just once more to let it be known which of the numerous cults or denominations is authorized to speak for Him? The Jews, of course, put that claim in several thousand years ago, but so have many others before and after they did. God, it is claimed, has revealed Himself on a great number of occasions, not only to high-level leaders and teachers like the patriarchs, Moses, Jesus, Mahommed, but also to lesser lights like prophets and saints. God also took many occasions to communicate through satellites, such as angels of various importance. All that exists as guidance on the subject of the divine essence is hearsay—claims of numerous cults of thousands of years ago. Then why does He not appear just once more, in the more recent and more enlightened era?

If we cannot find an explanation for the paradox in theology, rational thinking supplies it easily. God, to the rationalist and modern thinker, is that sublime force that speaks and reveals himself only through Nature. The laws of Nature are His laws, and to comprehend them, one must learn them through science. Therefore, God's true priests and ministers are the scientists, who consecrate themselves to the study of the laws and secrets of Nature. To take the next logical step, the way to serve God is to observe and conform to these laws.

It follows therefore, that the modern, enlightened Jew must give of his time and substance to set up a vanguard for the dissemination and spread of the principles and ideals briefly suggested in this chapter. An exact program and technique need not be attempted at this time. By merely pointing out the mental and ideological incongruities in the prevailing religious thinking and practices, the path and means for change and revision will suggest themselves. One approach may be the dialectic through essays, books, and lectures, and also the organization of groups or the joining of existing groups that are hospitable to new and forward looking ideas. One of the main tasks, however, and probably the first, will be attacking a major rampart: the inhibition against reexamination and analysis of ancient writings and teachings, only because of their supposedly sacred emanations. The first may well be the Old Testament itself.

CHAPTER V

REVISE THE BIBLE? WHY NOT?

1

The above query is put in timorous form and mood because the average person trembles at the profane implications of the question. One must indeed be bold and brazen to question the canonization of either the Old or New Testament. Yet there is a vast body of Bible criticism, higher and lower, wherein great scholars in the 17th, 18th, and 19th centuries dared question the text and many events related in the Bible, as well as their interpretations.

If, therefore, some of these eminent theologians had the temerity to delete and revise by interpretation some portions of the Bible, why should Jewish people feel squeamish about calling attention to contradictions and some unedifying portions of the Bible? Why should they not offer suggestions that would ennoble and exalt their God concept and elevate the stature of the Godhead to conform to their imagination and expectation of His greatness?

The first step will be to examine what certain discoveries have shown about the origin of the Bible, and then to call attention to some incongruities and vagaries evident in them.

2

Since the accidental discovery of the Rosetta Stone in Egypt in 1798, by a French Officer in Napoleon Bonaparte's military expedition, which supplied the key to the mysteries of antiquity, numerous excavations, expeditions and researches that followed threw much light on Biblical history. One of the latest and most successful of such contributions was made by Samuel Noah Kramer, associate curator of the University of Pennsylvania Museum, for which he received the John F. Lewis prize from the American Philosophical Society. From a collection of recordings on clay of the sacred writings of the Sumerians, who antedated the Babylonians, he established the original sources of the Old Testament. Kramer built his work on revelations based on deciphered inscriptions on clay tablets recovered from the mounds that now mark the buried ancient cities of Babylon. The first of these tablets was deciphered by George Smith, the English archeologist, over 50 years ago. It presented a story of the sacred books of Babylon that closely parallels the story of the flood, as recorded in the Book of Genesis. These tablets came from the Library of King Asharbanipal, who reigned in Babylon in the seventh century B.C. Other parts of the story were inscribed for and have been recovered from the library of the great Babylonian King Hammurabi, who reigned prior to 1500 B.C. Much of the contents of these early Babylonian sacred writings appears in Hebrew sacred books.

That all this lore should have passed to the Jews during their sojourn in their Babylonian exile in 572 is as simple as adding two and two. The average intelligent person is, therefore, confronted with this dilemma: he must choose between the supernatural theory of the divine origin of the collection of books apocryphal in source and authorship, differing in style and contradicting known facts, or the laboriously built up scientific accounts of the origin of these books. For one not tied to dogma and superstition, the decision is both easy and obvious. It is most deplorable that the precedent set by good Father Abraham in boldly smashing the silly idols of his ancestors and bravely proclaiming monotheism, could not be emulated by some of our enlightened religious leaders. They left that role to a forward-looking, pioneering branch of Christianity—the Unitarians. No wonder so many Jews flock to that church. It seems that our conventional Jewish pulpit missed the opportunity of continuing in the vanguard of religious leadership. However, it is comforting to know that while organized Jewish theology "missed the boat" on real and true reform in respect to the theory and philosophy of religion, Jewish laity continued to this day the Jewish tradition and passion for social reform and betterment, so amply and fully manifested by the ancient Prophets. Will there arise in Jewish religious leadership someone, or a group, who will rescue its

theology from the mire of outdated superstition and silly sophistry? Only the future can give the answer. It is high time for
such a phenomenon.

3

It would be a Herculean task to explore thoroughly the Old
Testament for contradictions and unedifying portions requiring
revision or deletion. However, by way of a few illustrations, we
will direct attention to some, to indicate what we are driving at.

Let us start at the fountainhead, the Ten Commandments.
How many people would consider it proper to fling the charge of
jealousy at one another? How many would proclaim their own
jealousy, even if down deep in their hearts they knew themselves
to be jealous? Yet the Second Commandment places God in that
humiliating position.

Here are some passages that compromise, to say the least, God's
reputation and place Him in a dubious, self-contradictory position. First, He is represented as a God of Justice and Truth:

God of truth and without iniquity, just and right is He. (Deuteronomy
XXXII-4.)
I am the Lord which exercises loving kindness, judgment and righteous-
ness on the earth, for in these things I delight. (Jeremiah IX-24.)
Shall not the Judge of all the earth do right? (Genesis XVIII-25.)

Then He turns into a jealous, unjust, and embittered God:

For I the Lord, thy God, am a jealous God, visiting iniquity of the fathers
upon the children unto the third and fourth generations. (Exodus XX-5.)
Cursed be Canaan; a servant of servants shall be he unto his brethren.
(Genesis IX-25.)

He is a God of Peace, but He is even more a God of War:

The Lord is a man of war. (Exodus XV-3.)
The Lord of Hosts is His name. (Isaiah LI-15.)

He is a merciful, tender God:

For His mercy endureth forever. (1 Chronicles XVI-34.)

But He is also a vindictive, destructive, and vengeful God:

[98]

The Lord, thy God, is a devouring fire and a jealous God. (Deuteronomy IV-24.)

Because they looked into the Ark of the Lord, even He smote of the people fifty thousand and three score and ten men. (I Samuel XV-2, 3.)

The Lord, thy God, cast down great stones from heaven upon them—and they died. (Joshua X-11.)

Now go and smite Amelek, and utterly destroy all that they have, and spare them not, but slay both men and women, infant and suckling. (Samuel SV-2, 3.)

What delectable sentiments to charge to God! Killing is forbidden:

Thou shalt not kill. (Exodus XX-13.)

but try to reconcile it with:

Thus saith the Lord, God of Israel: Put every man his sword by his side and go in and out from gate to gate throughout the camp and slay every man his brother, and every man his companion, and every man his neighbor. (Exodus XXXII-27.)

and:

So Jehu slain all that remained of the house of Ahab . . . And the Lord said unto Jehu: Because thou hast done well in executing that which is right in mine eyes, and hast done unto the house of Ahab according to all that was in my heart, thy children of the fourth generation shall sit on the throne of Israel. (11 Kings X-11-30.)

This may have been good ethics in the days when it was written. But can you love the Lord for it today?

It is difficult to conceive that any normal person of average intelligence in this age could condone the blood-curdling, barbarous deeds that are attributed to God Himself in the above quotations. His directions as to the treatment of Amelek and his people is exactly in line with the treatment of Hitler's victims. It is more than likely that in the conflict with Amelek the tender treatment prescribed reflected the sentiments of the embattled, outraged, and enraged participants in the conflict; but to perpetuate it as "holy writ" and charge it to God Himself is nothing but sheer blasphemy. How could a follower of Twentieth Century humanities possibly honor a deity who utters such vile and brutal directions?

[99]

There are similar contradictions in the dealings with the Hivites. How can anyone be credulous or blind enough to approve and consider sacred the perfidious treatment of the Hivites by the sons of Jacob? Prince Shechem of the Hivites fell in love with Dinah, sister of the sons of Jacob, and took possession of her. After vigorous remonstrances, the sons of Jacob became reconciled to the marriage and agreed to accept Shechem as their brother-in-law, on condition that he submit to circumcision and prevail on his townsmen to do the same. Shechem accepted this condition, had himself circumcised, and compelled his townsmen to do likewise. But on the third day after the operation, when the brothers knew that the Hivites were incapable of resistance or self-defense, they fell upon them and slaughtered them to a man. Even their own father, Jacob, denounced the outrage. (Genesis XXXIV, 2-30.)

Another illustration is the unedifying episode of the treatment of Esau by his brother Jacob and the unpleasant complicity of the mother, Rachel, in the scheme to deprive the older brother of his birthright. (Genesis XXVII, 1-27.)

There is also the treacherous and foul murder of the priests and prophets of Baal by Jehu after a pledge of safety was given. (II Kings X, 18-28.)

One of the most obscene passages to be found in any book is the incident of Onan refusing, through withdrawal, to allow his brother's widow to become pregnant by him, a contrary action to his father's clear instructions. The crowning absurdity and blasphemy of this incident is that Onan so enraged God by this act that God slew him. (Genesis XXXVIII, 8-10.)

The instance where Lot's daughters provoked him to commit incest furnishes another example of impropriety. (Genesis XIX, 31-36.)

Had all the writings that make up the Old Testament been passed down like any other collection of ancient manuscripts, one could regard it just as a record of a barbarous age, to be accepted or rejected. But one dares not do that with the Bible. Canonization and the seal of sacredness precludes it, for all that is recorded therein is sanctified as the quintessence of logic, wisdom, and justice. It is the "word of God." To cast the slightest doubt or aspersion, no matter how mild, is heresy, to be punished by eternal perdition. Indeed, in other times and places, men were burned at the stake or tortured or excommunicated for saying a good deal less than is risked here.

In a friendly discussion with a lay Hebrew scholar, I pointed out some of these contradictions and incongruities in the Bible, and his reply was that the Talmud, especially the Midrash, takes out all of these inconsistencies by interpreting them as symbolism, and in this manner it reconciles them with modern thought. This apologia gives rise to the question: Why, in the first place, plant conundrums and absurdities, which call for endless exposition and discussion? The difficulty about these long expositions and discussions is that not one person of this generation in a thousand (except scholars) has either the time, or inclination, or the qualifications to delve into Midrash; the one in a thousand who might undertake such a task would have to devote his entire life to dig in and peruse the Talmud to reconcile and solve the jigsaw puzzle.

One wonders what possible good is the inclusion of the unsavory and unedifying incidents herein pointed out, and thousands of similar ones, in a work like the Old Testament. What purpose could they possibly serve? But to ask this is to imply that the Bible should have been edited, and that, from the theological point of view, is treason—a betrayal of religion.

4

A person of even average intelligence in modern times likes to visualize his God as the one who is all-powerful, all-just, and all-wise, incomparably superior to any human or celestial force. How, then, can one reconcile these antics ascribed to Him, and the thousands of other contradictions, throughout the vast body of canonized religious writings? Is there any common sense or dignity in most of the prayers parroted in the synagogues and temples, prayers wherein God is flattered, cajoled, and offered bribes in a fashion that an intelligent, self-respecting person would resent? Indeed, it is doubtful whether the average worshiper would not feel sheepish and abashed at the things he fervently recites, were they in the vernacular. Nor, I suggest, could the most conceited prima donna, or the most incorrigible egomaniac, listen to the never-ending supplications, pleas, and sycophantic adulation offered up to God daily by the practicing religionists in their prayers.

Man is God's noblest creation. No theologian will deny that. Quite the contrary, he will enthusiastically proclaim that. Yet, while he will admit the right and necessity of man to breathe, eat, and drink in order to live and thrive and exercise all normal functions that nature endowed him with and intended him to exercise, he must by his thinking, shut out part of his mind and close his eyes to certain things. He must not, for instance, ask how it is that an omnipotent, omniscient, and omnipresent deity, who ordains and rules everything in the world, can visit punishment and destruction on the creatures he shaped and formed? One of the principal prayers during the Jewish high holidays, Rosh Hashona and Yom Kippur, is known as "Insana Toikef." In it is written, and with much fervor and glow recited by every worshiper, that all the happenings for the coming year are recorded during Rosh Hashona and sealed on Yom Kippur. Everyone's fate is preordained in detail at the beginning of the year. This not only implies but definitely means that all the outrages against millions of children and innocent men and women during world wars or normal times were decreed by some celestial synod and approved by God himself. "There is nothing willed on earth that is not willed in Heaven."

This does not mean one should belittle or ridicule the Bible. It is a monumental work, and the religions based on it great institutions. The Old Testament alone consists of thirty-nine books and took some ten centuries for its compilation. That is the belief not only of historians and scientists, but of most enlightened theologians. The Bible—the Old and New Testaments—wielded tremendous power in shaping civilization and will continue to do so for a long time to come. It provides all the more reason to study both, but not to be the dupes of either. We must regard the Bible as a priceless collection of folk culture and myths, in which are interwoven the history and art of primitive and ancient peoples before the genius for orderly expression was developed. Undoubtedly, it contains great gems of literary and artistic value. They should be preserved, treasured, and studied, but not worshiped.

CHAPTER VI

THE SEPHARDIC AND ASHKENAZIC TRADITIONS

Delineation of Ashkenazic and Sephardic Judaism is not limited to differences in ritual, "minhagim" (religious customs) or order of prayer and Hebrew accents and pronunciation. Other differences are much more basic and deeper. Their respective world outlooks, tendencies, and philosophies were at opposite poles. It is true that the period of glory and achievement of the Sephardic Jews ended a couple of centuries ago, and that the productive era of the Ashkenazic Jews is only now tapering off, though their influence and vogue may continue for an indeterminate period. But in a century from now (not a long time in a historic sense) Ashkenazic Jews may be as rare and few as the Sephardic are now. It does not follow that, in the aggregate, there will be fewer Jews. There may indeed be more, but the Ashkenazic tradition will either have undergone a great change or have completely faded out. However, regardless of the fact that Sephardic Jews have largely disappeared from the Jewish scene today or that the Ashkenazic Jews may change or disappear a century hence, the attitudes and ideas they each stood for, will not disappear. Indeed, they may even take on greater importance.

In history it is not infrequent that movements, organizations and names disappear, but the currents and forces behind them continue under different forms. Jewish history itself furnishes a perfect illustration. While to the modern student "Sadducees and Pharisees" are names of two ancient parties or groupings among Jews, the underlying principles and differences of that day are pretty much the same as those that divide Jewish thinking in modern times.

So, in perspective, it is not too important that Sephardic Jews are near the point of extinction, and that nearly all religious Jews of this era are Ashkenazic. What is important is that the differences in their thinking, ideas, and world outlook are as valid and important today as ever before. Regardless of the identification of individual Jews with one or another religious grouping, their mental and emotional reactions and loyalties, in the main, follow the same channels as those that divided the Sephardim and Ashkenazim.

Thus far, history's verdict, from the standpoint of the progressive and rationalist, gives the edge to the Sephardic "way of life." The great Jewish historian Graetz reports: "Whether from fancy or pride, it was supposed that . . . Sephardic Jews were the posterity of the noblest tribe, and included among them descendants in direct line from King David; hence the Jews looked upon them as a kind of Jewish nobility." (*History of the Jews,* Vol. 4, page 382.)

Any impartial evaluation will concede the important contribution the Sephardic Jews made to civilization in being the chief transmitter of the culture of the Orient, which also included ancient Greek culture, to the West. In that alone they perhaps made possible, and certainly accelerated, the great Renaissance in Europe. Their creative contribution to Judaism and to Jewish literature has probably never been excelled in Jewish post-exilic history. Moses Maimonides and Judah Halevi are merely the top names in a galaxy of leaders in every field of religious, cultural, scientific, and political endeavor, which created the golden era in Spanish Jewish history.

If this be deemed a somewhat partisan view in favor of Sephardic Jews, let us summon a modern, brilliant, and imaginative writer who, though proclaiming his partisanship for the Ashkenazic Jews, gives an objective appraisal of the two. In a scholarly and brilliant article (*Commentary,* May, 1948, page 416), Professor Abraham J. Heschel, of the Jewish Theological Seminary of New York, traces the two great traditions in Jewish history, the Sephardic and Ashkenazic. He shows that the Sephardic originated with the Spanish Jews. From there, through emigration and expulsion, they spread along the Mediterranean coast and to Holland, England, and other communities in Western Europe. As for the Ashkenazic trend, he traces it to Jews who originally came from Babylon and Palestine and drifted into the Balkans and central and eastern Europe. It is they who evolved the Yiddish language and literature. In a masterly series of abstract vignettes, he outlines and defines the two great traditions and their course and influence on Judaism. Their sharp con-

trasts and contradictions are shown with admirable objectivity,
sympathy and understanding. This is all the more commendable
since the writer himself appears to be a strong adherent of the
Ashkenazic tradition.

Based alone on this article and the presentation it makes, this
writer is, with equal definiteness, on the side of the Sephardic
tradition, despite (or perhaps because of) the fact that his forebears belonged to the Ashkenazic group. To him there is something solid, constructive, and plausible in the Sephardic attitude
and way of life. According to Professor Heschel, the Spanish Jews,
products of the Sephardic school, "were responsible for the earlier
brilliant epoch in Jewish history, distinguished not only by monumental scientific achievements, but also by a universality of spirit
. . . they often seemed to emphasize the elements Juadism had in
common with classical philosophy to the neglect of its own
specific features." On the other hand, the Ashkenazic system
developed in "isolation, grew out of its own ancient roots in an
indigenous environment, independent of the trends and conven-
tions of the surrounding world." The Ashkenazi adhered tenaciously to their own traditions, and they concentrated on cul-
tivating without borrowing from other cultures. In this, they
were totally impervious and indifferent to outside opinion. On
the other hand, the achievements of the Sephardic Jews in medi-
cine and astronomy "contributed greatly to the development of
European civilization as a whole." It may be added parentheti-
cally that by the same token, the achievements of the Ashkenazic
Jews contributed to their isolation.

In the following paragraphs Professor Heschel places in
juxtaposition the distinguishing features of the two traditions:

Here, in the Ashkenazic realm, the amalgamation of Torah and Israel was
accomplished. Ideals became folkways, divine imperatives a human concern,
the people itself became a source of Judaism, a source of spirit. The most
distant became very intimate, very near. Spontaneously, without external
cause, the people improvised customs of celestial solemnity. The dictates of
feeling were heeded as commandments of highest authority. Jews began to
know what it means: "From within my flesh do I see the Lord."

Sephardic books are distinguished by their strict logical arrangement. They
are composed according to a clear plan; every detail has its assigned place,
and the transitions from one subject to another are clear and simple. Ashkenazic writers forego clarity for the sake of depth. The contours of their
thoughts are irregular, vague, and often perplexingly entangled; their con-

tent is restless, animated by inner wrestlings and a kind of baroque emotion.

Sephardic books are like Raphaelesque paintings; Ashkenazic books like the works of Rembrandt, profound, allusive and full of hidden meanings. The former favor the harmony of a system, the latter the tension of dialectic; the former are sustained by solemnity, the latter by impulsive inspiration. The strength of the Sephardic scholars lies in their mastery of expression, that of the Ashkenazic in the unexpressed overtones of their words. A spasm of feeling, a passionate movement of thought, an explosive enthusiasm will break through the form.

The Sephardim aspired to personal perfection and attempted to express their ideas rationally. They strove for tranquility of soul, for inner peace and contentment. Their ethics were at time bourgeois, full of prudence and practical wisdom. To follow the golden rule, to take the middle course and avoid extremes, was one of their most popular maxims. The Cabala remained the pursuit of the few; in contrast to the situation in Eastern Europe, the life of the people in the Sephardic community was hardly touched by the bold mystic doctrines of some of its rabbis.

But Ashkenazic ethics knows no perfection that is definable; its vision aimed at the infinite. Never compromising, never satisfied, always striving; "Seek higher than that." The Ashkenazic moralist or Hassid was exalted; he yearned for the transcendental, the preternatural. He somehow felt that not only space, but also the soul was endless. Not for him the tranquil contemplation, the gradual ascent. What he sought was boundless fervor, praying and learning without limit or end. For though the seeker is engaged in a persistent struggle with the material and infinite and cannot escape himself permanently, he can at least aspire to divest himself, in short moments of ecstacy, of all earthly concerns.

To the writer, the Ashkenazic mind, as depicted in the above paragraphs, presents a psychopathic mentality, a mind in a wild flight of occult exaltation into a mystical and celestial sphere bordering on the abnormal. His feet are on the earth, but his head is in the clouds. All thought of the practical, human phase of life is on the periphery of his existence, and an unavoidable and disagreeable necessity. The substance and real joy of living is in his relations with the Deity in the hereafter. Thus evolved the ghetto mentality, exemplified by the Hassidim with their crude superstition, and the "Tzadick" or miracle-working rabbi. Many are the apologia for this benighted and baneful influence on a large segment of Eastern Jews in the Diaspora. The principal thesis is that Hassidism was a form of escape from the unbearable miseries and tortures of ghetto life. But to exalt and glamorize it as something beautiful in itself strains the imagination. It is clear that those who now rhapsodize over it and sing its praises never lived with it, but reacted vicariously through the partisan poetic vision of its acolytes. What we need is a modern Cervantes to expose its absurdities and ridiculous pretensions.

There is a bottomless gulf between these two traditions in Jewish life. The Ashkenazi accepted an anthropomorphic deity as the special god of Israel who, at the same time, is the universal God. Their assumption was that the Jews are his favored and special people, and, by implication at least, the rest of humanity takes second place. In recognition of this privileged position, their ancestors assumed the burden of spreading and disseminating the laws and principles of the Torah and the other sacred writings. Their sole and exclusive function in this life is consecration and devotion to God through prayer, fasting, self-denial, self-flagellation, and the ceaseless study of the Torah, as well as the observance of all laws and ordinances. All this is only a prelude to eternal life in the hereafter. The physical and secular interests, inclinations, and aspirations of the Jew are to be subordinated, or entirely suppressed, if they clash with religious duties. That is the *raison d'être* of the Jew and the real meaning of his life.

The Sephardim, on the other hand, seem to have made a conspicuously satisfactory beginning to veer away from this parochial view and adopt one more in harmony with the exigencies of life. Thus, as Professor Heschel admits, while serving God, they make their contributions to life and civilization. Moreover, they exert themselves to the incomparably nobler task of building a bridge of understanding with their fellow men of other persuasions, thereby lessening theological differences and promoting peace and happiness—an end to be preferred above the isolation and mysticism of the Ashkenazi.

The elements in American Jewry imbued with the teachings of Moses Mendelssohn, Abraham Geiger, Isaac M. Wise, and others, who were the exponents and founders of the Reform Movement, were definitely yielding to the Sephardic tradition. However, the holocaust in Jewish life fomented by Nazi Germany, and the chaos and disorganization in Europe during and after the Second World War, brought into Jewish life a reactionary chauvinism and hysteria. It resulted in a spectacular boost for the Ashkenazic teachings and practices, which afforded an escape in isolationism and mysticism. The Reform Movement under this influence felt compelled to restore some of the older traditional practices, such as the services of a cantor, the building of a token succoth (tabernacle), and similar concessions. This trend, however, is bound to disappear with the return of normal conditions in Jewish life. When that comes about, the thinking, progressive element will return, and will once again turn their faces toward growth and emancipation from superstition.

Indeed, it is hoped that this emancipation will bring the next logical step to free Jewish theology from the medievalism of not only the Talmud but the belief in a personal Deity, who revealed Himself in a physical sense and made His wishes known. It is high time that Jews take the next step and recognize that the Supreme Creator manifests Himself only through his work in Nature and that His only laws are the natural laws. Let the Jewish people resume their place in the world as the leaders in ethics and religion.

Some believers in a liberal religion fear that it cannot offer a substitute for the many beautiful customs and practices in liturgical services and ceremonies and for the celebration of many holidays. A strong nostalgia for these prevails. The answer is that all liturgical services and celebration of holidays can be continued. By cleansing them of the dross of superstition and giving them a poetic setting, these services can be continued in an even more beautiful atmosphere. In a similar manner, the great literary gems of the Old Testament and of the world's great literature can be given appropriate readings at religious services, in place of the repetitious, childish fawning on God that characterizes nearly all the prayers in vogue today.

CHAPTER VII

PAGANISM AND JUDEO-CHRISTIAN IDEOLOGY

1

For a clearer understanding of the points and arguments in the following chapter, a few observations should be made on semantics—the use of power of words and language. Semantics is one of the few arts that is also coming to be recognized as a science. Through the mastery of the spoken word, thousands of men in every era and clime reached the highest pinnacle of leadership and power. The written word has given the world the greatest masterpieces of literature. By the same token, semantics, like other arts and sciences, can be, and is at times, employed for evil purposes. The venal politician, the propagandist in subversive movements, the rabble-rouser, the high-pressure salesman, the diplomat specializing in the art of double-talk and sophistry, are illustrations. All these prove the correctness of a cynicism attributed to Voltaire—that the function of words is to conceal the thought of the speaker.

Literature, the written word, supplied semantics with even greater ramifications in wider fields both for good and evil. The classics in history, poetry, belles-lettres and science, demonstrate the artistry, skill, and effects of semantics. Certain national traits are also disclosed. Some of the greatest German classicists, scientists, philosophers and economists, with their German language and its long, involved sentences, have shown a deplorable ineptness in semantics. For example, take Immanuel Kant, with his *Categorical Imperative, Critique of Pure Reason,* and *Critique of Judgment;* Frederick Hegel, with his *Thesis, Antithesis and Synthesis,* Arthur Schopenhauer with his *The World of Will and Idea* and *Nirvana,* and even Karl Marx and his *Das Kapital.* These and many others like them have caused mental dyspepsia to generations.

On the other hand, many English classicists have shown an

innate and natural aptitude for semantics. Herbert Spencer's works are relatively easy and palatable reading, as are David Hume's. So is Darwin's *Origin of Species* and his other works. Jurisprudence, which is generally recognized as a dry subject, especially for the layman, is presented in such a fascinating and compelling style in Blackstone's *Commentaries* that it has become a literary classic. Similar examples in the realm of history are Gibbon's *Decline and Fall of Rome,* Buckle's *History of Civilization in England;* and the brilliant classic in one volume by Winwood Reade, *The Martyrdom of Man.* Other illustrations might be given ad infinitum, but space will not permit.

Semantics was sometimes resorted to for symbolism, either as a possible shield against political persecution and reprisal, or for artistic effect. Swift's great satire, *Gulliver's Travels,* is an illustration of the first and *Penguin Island,* by Anatole France, the second.

But a more ancient and extravagent use of the art—even before its classification as an art or science and before it was called semantics—was made by the mystics, both among Jews and Christians. They not only indulged in anonymity but employed a style that offered the greatest latitude in evasiveness and double-talk. The pattern for that style was most likely set by the ancient priests of Egypt and those of Mount Olympus in Ancient Greece. It was a matter of expedience for them. It was part of their business to predict coming events, and they had to invent an elastic and subtle form in order to be able to twist their meaning to the ultimate facts.

The later mystics made use of this method, as well as of allegory and symbolism. It suited their purpose perfectly. It was frequently used by the writers of the Old and the New Testaments, and also by the Jewish Prophets. Here are just a few illustrations. Joseph's interpretation of Pharoah's dreams (see Exodus), Daniel, Job and Jonah. A brief and popularized vignette on the use of symbolism is the "Had Gadye" in the Passover Hagadah. At times, however, such efforts were crude and vulgar; an example of this is the attempt to equate the sensuous, lyrical description of physical love and passion in the "Song of Songs" with the relations between God and Israel—an allegory wherein God is the lover, and Israel the maiden.

But those who reveled to their hearts' content in both symbolism and mystic cabalistic double-talk are the authors of the Talmud. This method is still much in vogue in modern theological dialecticism and Hassidic literature. An example is furnished in a recent article by Will Herberg (*Commentary*, May, 1949, page 453): "The feeling for tension in the human situation appears strikingly in Buber's interpretation of the Messianic vision. 'Redemption,' he says, 'occurred forever and none has ever occurred'; the kingdom of God is here among us as a power and a summons and yet always remains as the promise of fulfillment at the 'end of the days.' Out of this polarity of the 'already and the not yet,' is generated the dynamic of spiritual life." Try, if you can, to reconcile or decipher the meaning of "occurs forever and none has ever occurred" and "the already and the not yet"! If the unfairness of lifting a quotation from its context is suggested, then let the reader consult the article itself or, better still, try and get his teeth into the morass of the original Buber source, or, for that matter, in most of Buber's writings. Another example from the same article is this by Paul Tillich: "Perfection is an eschatological conception, an impossible possibility." The writings of Kafka are another illustration.

For the purpose of our thesis, this introduction of semantics could have been abbreviated, or entirely eliminated, except for the fact that a wider background of the power and function of words tends to bring out more clearly the dubiousness and evasiveness in present-day discussions of theological issues. Such are the economic, political, and social pressures in our day that many journalists, publicists, and philosophers who have iconoclastic or unorthodox views on theology, nationalism or other vital issues employ the shifty, involved, and cloudy phrase so as not to run the risk of being pinned down. This makes for confusion and bewilderment. The writer, fortunately being free from such pressures and consciously defying the inhibitions of taking an unpopular position (some will denounce it as brazen), dares to pose the issue between so-called Paganism (alias Hellenism) and the Judeo-Christian ideology.

To what degree Judeo-Christian literature succeeded in discrediting the civilization of the Ancient Greeks and Romans—often referred to as the age of Paganism—can be seen from the fact that the very term or word paganism is one of opprobrium. To call one a pagan is the same as calling him an outcast or a scoundrel. Yet, we know that in the historical sense, Paganism stands for a way of life. In its narrow sense, it connotes a plurality of deities, in contradistinction to the Judaic one-God-monotheism. In its wider scope, however, it represents a political and social system that prevailed in the more potent and fruitful half of the ancient world for something like thirteen or fourteen centuries.

It is of interest to place in juxtaposition these two great systems—the Judeo-Christian and Pagan. They originated on opposite sides of the Mediterranean: the one east and the other west, and not far apart in point of time. The Biblical reckoning of the world's existence, by which is really meant the period when mankind began to be hazily conscious and articulate, is somewhat under sixty centuries. But inasmuch as, according to the Bible itself, little happened in the first ten or fifteen centuries, until the advent of the Patriarchs, it brings it down to about the period of the awakening of Ancient Greece. At any rate, that is about the time when Abraham destroys the idols of clay and wood, symbols of paganism, and proclaims monotheism. This, on the authority of the Bible itself, is the point of demarcation, the parting of the ways between Paganism and the Judeo system.

Therefore, the issue is: What contribution did each make toward civilization and the betterment of mankind?

Let us inquire into the character of the Greek-Roman world and that of their satellites that emerged and developed on the west side of the Mediterranean. The first important factor in the lives of the early Greeks and Romans was that through lack of a central deity, divine authority was of necessity divided among numerous gods who competed with one another, despite the fact that each was supposed to preside over a different jurisdiction. It inevitably followed that these deities were placed on a lower pedestal and enjoyed less prestige than the one supreme God. Indeed, to the Ancient Greeks, the plural gods were little more than supermen, with many of the traits and afflictions of ordinary human beings. In the main, they exercised no great terror over the minds of their subjects, nor were many taboos and inhibitions created by these gods. The result was that this relative freedom from fear and superstition gave full and free play to the minds and imagination of the early Greeks. Little wonder that there flowed from them a colorful and glorious civilization.

We cannot deviate too much to dwell on the details of this vital and far-reaching development of their civilization, except to point briefly to a few of their major achievements. The Greeks gave the world such great philosophers as Thales, Anaximander, Anixemenes, Pythagoras, and Parmenides (probably the first to lay down the rule to employ reason and sensory impressions in philosophical speculation). In addition, they gave the world that celebrated philosophical trinity, Socrates, Plato and Aristotle, who today, twenty-four centuries later, are still regarded as beacon lights by modern students in that field.

They were likewise pre-eminent in literature, though it is also true that Egyptian, Babylonian, Assyrian and Hebraic literature preceded theirs. But there was this important difference: the latter dealt mainly with ecclesiastical matters, and the former, although giving a good deal of space to the antics of their gods, devoted greater attention to the foibles and problems of human beings.

In the fields of science, the arts, architecture, sculpture, poetry and music, the Greeks were without peer. Above all, they gave full and free flight and scope to their minds and imagination in the art of living. They introduced sanitation and public and private baths, and promoted and encouraged the development and perfection of the human body through gymnasiums and various kinds of sports. In this way they developed self-reliance and a free spirit. They encouraged thinking without inhibitions and gave free scope to reason, to inquiry, and to experiment— each a step in the direction of progress and the good life. Against these fine qualities, there stands the charge of their preoccupation with military activities and constant warring among themselves. The Spartans and Romans must bear much of the responsibility for the art, science, and prestige of militarism.

Now we shall glimpse briefly the almost simultaneous evolution of the Judeo-Christian world. The first phenomenon is that the priestly class took the masses in tow by means of an austere, somber religion. They split the human individual into two: the tangible physical body, and an intangible, indefinable, inscrutable thing called the "soul." By reserving complete control of this elusive "soul," the priesthood ingeniously retained a hostage for the discipline and control of the physical individual. They conjured up a terrifying force with human personality, attributes, and form, and named it "Jehovah," "Eloim," or "God"— "I AM THAT I AM." They contended that this new force is the only genuine god of the entire universe, in contrast to the phony gods of the Greeks. In His name, through Moses, the priests handed down, first, a brief and excellent code of laws or morals called the Ten Commandments. Later, they elaborated this into the Pentateuch or Five Books of Moses, wherein, at great length and in detail, the relations of man to God and man to man were defined, and there was set up a bulwark of inhibitions and taboos which constrict the natural impulses and cravings of the human heart. If further expansion of these laws had stopped with the Pentateuch, it might have been possible for posterity somehow to balance and regulate their lives to conform to its numerous ordinances and requirements. But, later, generations of priests and ecclesiastics continued to pile up scripture upon scripture and enshrine them as sacred, although they were a few notches below the Ten Commandments and the Pentateuch. Thus, the Old Testament was completed. Then came a rebellion or split, and a New Testament was formulated and laid the foundation for Christianity. As that movement grew apace, there was overlaid, by way of supplement, further and additional comment and interpretation of the Old Testament, which ultimately was formulated into the Talmud. Finally, it is alleged, the Scribes, through their leader Ezra, put an end to this continuous appendaging by the edict of canonization. The edict made all subsequent writings secular and profane and deprived them of their "sacred" privileges.

These sacred or canonized writings, together with all "non-sacred" subsequent works, prayers and sermons, enjoined everyone to "worship, fear, and serve" God. But the directions, interdictions, and proscriptions are so vast, bewildering, and conflicting that one cannot breathe without becoming a "sinner" by stepping on some of them. Had these writings emphasized social ethics—righteous conduct and attitude of man toward his fellow man—as the will of God and hence the essence of religion, it would have been a boon to the human race. Instead, the accent is on the appeasement of a terrifying, whimsical, mysterious God. The major purpose and mission of man on this Earth is to serve this God in the multitudinous and odd demands He makes; but, to meet these demands, one must subvert his nature in many respects. He must restrain his impulses, though they be normal and wholesome. "Ye go not about after your own heart and your own eyes, after which ye use to go astray." (Numbers 15-37) He must practice fasting and generally lead an ascetic life; he must restrain his natural curiosity, lest he question the ways of God and thus be guilty of blasphemy. Above all, he must spend his days and years in prayer and study drab, endless casuistry. (See *Basic Judaism*, pages 123-24, by Steinberg.) Over and above this, he must be harried by a fear-fixation that an ever-watchful deity is constantly on his trail for the slightest deviation, at the risk of jeopardy to his soul and perpetual damnation.

While not as cruel as that infamous Christian doctrine of "original sin," which plasters a guilt-fixation on every infant the moment it leaves the mother's womb, the Jewish neophyte lives in an atmosphere of mental and intellectual duress; he fears God's retribution in this life and worries about the fate of his soul in the hereafter. All this is in the name of high moral principles and on the pretense that an omnipotent God imposed rigid discipline on his frail and imperfect "chosen" creatures, who were to consecrate themselves and devote all of their energies to broadcasting God's virtues and prestige among the rest of the human beings. That looks like putting the cart before the horse. Common sense would suggest that an all-perfect, just, merciful and wise Creator would want his prize creation, man, to prosper physically, mentally and spiritually. To that end, God would ordain that man apply his energies toward art, culture, science, and the cultivation of the human graces, so that he may take pride in the things he performs. If one were to observe the facts of nature, the true method by which God manifests himself, and note its beauty and symmetry, and the abundant dependability of its supply of all things necessary for the sustenance and growth of humans, one would be convinced that God's purpose is that His creatures prosper and be happy. Yet, the clergy interprets God's will that man must cringe before Him, sing His praises in monotonous prayers, deny or limit full and natural expression, and, above all, deaden his mental faculties when it comes to questions of religion. Man must leave it all to the priests and rabbis.

In this respect, the clergy has had its way for these past twenty centuries. Out of it, what do we find? First, a split from Judaism and Christianity emerges. Six centuries later another break is effected and Mohammedanism arises. These three are forever feuding with each other, resulting in the desolation and slaughter of God's children and spreading chaos throughout the world. To make matters worse, these three religious branches splinter themselves into innumerable, lesser cults, credal factions and denominations that hate and despise each other with greater intensity and bitterness than the three original major factions.

[115]

For more than fifteen centuries there have been bloody clashes among these splintered denominations in religious wars that sacrificed the flower of mankind and brought misery, disease, and chaos in their wake. It would seem that the worst pagan institution, militarism, was the only heritage that Christianity took over.

It might have occurred to the enlightened and progressive mind that it would be a good idea if these two great systems, the Judeo-Christian and the Paganism of the Greeks and Romans, were to amalgamate, with the best features of each adopted. Happily, evolution has already performed that miracle. The Catholic hierarchy of the Middle Ages had its fling with its Crusades and the slave systems known as Feudalism and the Inquisition. The Renaissance was the inevitable reaction and revulsion to the barbarism of the Middle Ages. It broke through the darkness and brought with it the Paganism of the ancient Greeks—their culture, art, philosophy, science, and the humanities—all of which theology had banned. In the end, in a great measure, Hellenism or Paganism triumphed, although in the process Christian civilization became dualistic and schizophrenic. Theology will probably not admit it, but actually Christians are dividing their loyalties. They give lip service to the Church on Sundays, and the rest of the week they are pagans with a vengeance. Their phenomenal advance in the arts, sciences, humanities, and their commercial pursuits since the Renaissance fully demonstrate this. If anyone should regard that as an exaggerated evaluation, all he has to do is tune his ears to the lamentations of the clergy itself on the score of the paganistic practices and materialistic influences that prevail today.

Among the Jews, the metamorphosis is just as pronounced, despite the present resurgence of traditionalism. The early contact of Jews with Hellenism, or exposure to it, took place after the conquest of the Near East by Alexander the Great. From then on, the two ideologies clashed in different periods and places. At the present time, it would appear on the surface that old-fashioned religion and a good deal of fundamentalism has come back and is here to stay. But take a good look behind the marquee with its electric signs. Is there any resemblance between the modern up-to-date, luxurious synagogues, temples, and social centers, with their gyms, swimming pools and sports facilities, and the drab "Beth Hamidrash," the "Yeshivah," or even the "Great Synagogues" of the wealthier classes in the Europe of yesterday? To what extent does even the "awakened" present-day youth warm the hard benches in the houses of learning and pore into the large, heavy tomes of the Talmud? Indeed, how much observance is there today of the dietary laws and the rest of the 613 "mitzvahs," even by the zealous shouters for a return to traditionalism? There is very little. Jews, as well as Christians, give lip service to traditionalism on the Sabbath or holidays, simulate an interest in the sermons, and are pagans the rest of the week, pursuing their mundane ways, playing, feasting, attending concerts, the theatre, or following their scientific or cultural careers. Is this not what used to be denounced as Hellenism and the very negation of the Hassidic practices? Are there many who will deny that this is better living—a vast improvement in every sense over the life in the Ghetto or in the Middle Ages? If it exposes the inconsistency and hypocrisy of the two attitudes, well, what of it? After all, it is the purpose of discussions like this to try to reconcile differences, or, at least, to bring them to the surface and try to find some solution.

Both sides of this issue are set forth with admirable clarity and objectivity by the eminent scholar and historian, Dr. Abraham Leon Sachar, in his *A History of the Jews,* page 100. Here is the quotation:

The Hebraic and the Hellenic views of life have been often contrasted. The Hebrew stressed reliance upon an omnipotent God and conformity to a divinely sanctioned moral law; he was essentially serious, restrained, willing to recognize his finite limitations. To seek God was the ultimate wisdom, to follow His precepts the ultimate virtue. The Greek accepted no revelation as ultimate; he strove to penetrate the core of his conceptions, analyzing the very base of his knowledge. He was blessed with a delicate, subtle reason and with a keen desire to use it, to probe with it, to open the very heart of reality. The Hebrew was inclined to mysticism; he accepted the moral law and would not go beyond it. The Greek bowed to no law but that of complete self expression. He loved beauty and art, the outdoor life, and every aspect of nature which appealed to his aesthetic sensibilities. Where the Hebrew asked: "What must I do?" the Greeks asked "Why must I do it?" Matthew Arnold has put the difference between the two spirits in a series of famous epigrams. The uppermost idea with the Greek was to see things as they really are; the uppermost idea with the Hebrew was conduct and obedience. The Hebrew believed in the beauty of holiness, the Greek believed in the holiness of beauty.

The two points of view could not very well be reconciled in an individual. One could not accept a revealed law as ultimate, and yet honestly question the very foundation of life; or submit to a moral law and yet exploit one's capacities without restraint. But was it not possible for both spirits to be present in a whole people, residing in individuals who were splendid examples of each? National life would indeed be ideally rounded out if it developed at once the burning zeal for social righteousness of an Amos or an Isaiah, and the serene wisdom of a Socrates or a Plato, the moral fervour of a Jeremiah and the artistic genius of a Praxiteles.

CHAPTER VIII

LIFE AND RELIGION

1

The cardinal principle in nature, as it affects human beings and all other living things, is the instinct of self-preservation. That instinct contravenes and challenges many moral and ethical principles. It is on a parity with the theory of "original sin" among Christians, except that the instinct of self-preservation cannot be mollified or affected by holy water. It is nature's imperative, but in the wise ways of nature, that very same instinct becomes moral and benevolent. The same instinct which prompts a being to take the life of another living creature, or steal food or commit other depredations, can also be protective and benevolent toward its mate or offspring and will share everything with them. Nay, it will do more. It will cause a person to risk his own life to protect dear ones against an enemy. This is nature's shrewd way of renewing and perpetuating life. Indeed, it is the springboard for our highly developed and complicated civilization. All refinements in modern living began with it and were prompted by the desire to make things easier and better for those who depend on us; that, at least, is the ultimate purpose in our constant striving for improvement.

But it becomes necessary to look behind the instinct of self-preservation and examine some of its ramifications. We shall find, on further inquiry, that with some it can and does become more to be dreaded than "original sin." Its evaluation is beyond the knowledge of the profoundest minds. The good and evil in it lies in the extent, measure, and direction of its pursuit.

If it were not for that instinct, the fledgling would not acquire its protective feathers, learn to fly, or gather its food in order to survive. In humans, it is the same instinct that prepares the infant for the tasks of life. The child must go through many ordeals and arduous drillings of body and mind to meet the various exigencies of life. The measure of success in these preparations determines the success and fitness for future life. At this point, however, we are confronted by a human conundrum. With the birds or other creatures, when the period of preparation and training ends, and the young become self-reliant and capable of self-defense, that phase of their career is over. From then on, a great many other fortuitous factors determine how well they fare and their longevity—factors over which they have no or little control. Not so with *homo sapiens*. After the tortuous preparations for his career, and after acquiring the arts and wiles that fit him for life, the "instinct of self-preservation," which, at the start, is essential for survival, becomes predatory and over-extended and finally develops what may be called the "Croesus" or the "Napoleonic" complex, which, paradoxically, in the end often destroy him.

Let us clarify this with an illustration. Take a youth who prepares himself for a business, professional, or financial career. The incentive is security and happiness for himself and his dependents. When he has reached his goal and a satisfactory degree of proficiency in his field, enjoying ample remuneration and security, does he rest on his oars and thereafter take it easy? Does he broaden his life and make it more colorful and abundant through culture, social service, or through the many other channels that life offers? Some do, but they are the few and the exceptions. Most of the big "successes" or tycoons are not even aware when they have reached the peak of their careers, for by that time something else has entered their mental bloodstream. The virus called "ambition," the desire to excel and to rule, has taken possession of them. Only too often that virus distorts all other values in life. It's a single-track line that calls for the utmost concentration of every ounce of physical and mental energy, merely to hold on to the position they have attained. They find that they have chosen an extremely competitive world and are constantly being vigorously challenged by the younger generation, who, by virtue of being less weary and less blasé, have imagination and resourcefulness, and a fresher point of view. It is what Toynbee calls "challenge and response," except that the response of our "great man" is with hardened arteries and a shorter life. This is the "Croesus" complex. The other, a military version of the same complex, we call the "Napoleonic" complex. After all, government and the military have so far played a much greater role in the march of history than commerce and industry, which are of much more recent creation. Suppose, then, that one chooses the latter career, and after many years of back-breaking drilling and intense concentration finally "arrives" and "reaches" a degree of competence which assures him security, recognition, and a feeling that he has mastered his vocation. Does he rest on his laurels? Here, again, perhaps some do, but not many. For here, too, the virus of ambition sets in. In the short intervals that may be called "times of peace," those engaged in governmental careers, and more particularly those in military vocations, are submerged in what, for lack of a better term, may be styled "dynastic feuds and rivalries." These may have their dramatic or comic aspects but are never conducive to one's peace of mind. However, in times of a national emergency and world convulsion, they only too often become tragic to themselves and the rest of the nation.

The terms "Croesus" and "Napoleonic" complexes are peculiarly appropriate to bring out what is in the mind of the writer. The life, work, reputation, and tragic end of Croesus make him the prototype of all the financial and industrial tycoons since his day. The same holds true of military and royal tragedies before and after Napoleon. France, suffering for over a century from the oppression and abuse of irresponsible kings, a cruel and selfish upper class, and a fawning and indifferent clergy, finally exploded in an all-sweeping and destructive revolution. She found herself on an oasis in a European desert of monarchial reaction of the same type that the revolution exterminated. Three strong personalities attempted to direct the fate of the new People's Government—the celebrated Robespierre, Danton, and Murat. Each of them, in his own right, was afflicted with a "Napoleonic" complex; each aimed to rule or ruin. As it has done, and always does, to others so afflicted, it led to their tragic end. In this crisis, the original himself, Napoleon Bonaparte, made his appearance and became the savior of his country. As long as he remained loyal to them, the French were at his feet, and millions outside of France worshiped his name. Beethoven's alleged dedication of his "Eroica" to Bonaparte was only a manifestation of that spirit, even by the best and finest throughout Europe.

But did this mass-worship satisfy the megalomaniac? Just pause to contemplate how different world history would have been, and Napoleon's place in it, had he remained loyal and devoted to his people, who raised him from obscurity to greatness. He started with a commendable and noble impulse to rescue his nation in the hour of its trouble and despair. But the cursed virus "ambition" that entered his veins brought tragedy to himself, and, above all, to his people, and the world.

This writer has cited the career of Napoleon because of thousands of others before and after him, whose careers were similarly smashed and who brought ruin and misery to millions because they could not hold in check their accursed wild dreams of personal glory. The Stalin-Trotsky feud and the feud between Stalin and Tito are more recent illustrations.

2

Now note what the self-same complex did to theology, which should have protected and defended the people from the rich and from military tyrants. It may have seemed an irrelevant digression into economic and political history to discuss Croesus and Napoleon; but the purpose was to show that it is all of the same fabric and design, and that religion also followed similar patterns. After all, it is undeniable that the three great forces that kept the masses in check everywhere were the clergy, the military, and plutocracy, in the order of their historical appearance. (The thesis would be incomplete to name only religion and thus give it undue emphasis.) It is just to prove that the same human traits operated to make theology, known now as organized instituitional religion, the third arm of the ruling classes for the exploitation of the masses everywhere. It is fair to state that the early founders of the church, especially the martyrs, had different hopes and plans. Moreover, even today, there are many dissidents, who, if they had their way, would have religion play the role it always should have played as the power for light, healing, and peace. But one must evaluate and judge theology by the record it has made for itself, and not by what an inside minority would have it be. That record, unfortunately, is not good. It shows that while plutocracy used the economic necessity of the people to exploit them, and the military used fear of neighbor and necessity for defense against an enemy, thereby creating a rigid, anti-social caste, the clergy employed a more subtle and more successful method to enforce its exactions upon the public. It employed the occult power of superstition and magic—in short, it worked on the gullible through the mind.

The function of the church and religion per se was in the spiritual realm, to serve the masses with kindness, understanding, truth, and devotion. The people needed those who were qualified to aid and guide them in the solution of the many baffling problems and troubles that arose in their humble lives. This service was needed not only by individuals, but often by the group and nation. That had, indeed, been the hope of many of the early leaders and proponents of religion, such as Moses and Jesus, Thomas Aquinas, and many of their successors. Had this mission been realized, the honest religious leaders and teachers would have pursued the paths of research and inquiry that would have made them the pioneers in science and discovery, truth and culture. What humanity so desperately needed during its infancy was to be taken by the hand by its wise and benevolent leaders, and led out of ignorance and fear into the light of understanding, courage and uprightness. Then this world would surely have become a paradise. Unfortunately, nimble-witted adventurers climbed on the band wagon and seized the reins for their own nefarious schemes.

It early became clear to the theologians, whose realm is morals and ethics, that the crude discipline of the military, based on force, or the economic thumbscrews of the plutocrat would not serve their purpose. It must be something more subtle. They easily observed that the use of physical force, or duress, or economic power bred resentment and hatred, and there was always the potentiality of retaliation, if and when the wheel of fortune turned around. Through trial and error, it dawned on them that control of the mind of another is the surest, safest, and most endurable method. What one needed was a superior and keener intellect, and that was their stock in trade. Generally, that was the route to the profession, and their intellects were the tools with which they worked. They began by spinning yarns about spirits and ghosts, good and evil ones, that were a potent influence in molding the lives of human beings. The implication was always clear that the spinner of these yarns understood and could either manipulate or circumvent these shadowy forces. With this technique, they readily attained their ends. They won the battle without much struggle because they were not hampered by scruples or principles. Like so many of their type, they entrenched themselves by investing religion with superstition and supernaturalness, shrouding it in mysticism and making of it an esoteric movement. In this fashion, they perpetuated and insulated their sway over the common people. Instead of using understanding and simplicity in the service of truth, they threw up roadblocks in the mental growth of the people to prevent their understanding, so that it would be easier to control and exploit them.

An apt illustration of this is the birth and growth of the science of astronomy among the Egyptians. The fertility of the Nile delta sustained a heavy population, but continuity of the fertility was dependent on many natural factors, such as periodic inundation from the tropical rains which irrigated the delta. Some of the keener and more observant among them took note of these factors and were able to prognosticate and warn the population whether the food crops would be good and in abundance. They became the stargazers, and the first astronomers, meteorologists and engineers to build dykes and reservoirs. As possessors of such knowledge, they wielded great influence and power. They, in time, formed a clique and called themselves priests. They gave the impression that their knowledge came to them through special divine gifts, and that they had contact with the gods and could influence them. They made astronomy an esoteric science. The kings were quick to enter into an understanding with the priests, the result of which was the exploitation and oppression of the people. Thus, a set of orderly, natural facts became a weapon of power and mystery in the hands of an unscrupulous class, who used it to promote their own interests.

In similar fashion and with like methods, the leaders of these great religions assiduously planted the belief that they were in closer contact with, and understood the supernatural forces that rule this earth, and that God, the chief of these forces, made them His vicars to interpret and execute His will. Had they used their unique opportunity and influence to restrain the rapaciousness of the oppressors of the masses, to promote justice and defend the weak and poor, they would have been the true and undisputed leaders of humanity. Instead, they entered the vulgar competitive market for power, engaging in conflict with the other classes for temporal control. They were not content with spiritual prestige, but reached out for material mastery. They erected heavy ramparts of dogma and ritual, interfered in the fiscal domain of kings, set up claims for extraordinary rights and privileges, and thereby split the world into many cults, parties, and religious denominations. They conjured up a "hereafter" with a heaven and hell, and used it as a club over their followers to compel obedience. They gained further dominion over the mind of man by claiming to control his soul and conscience. This, with the aid of ritualism, assured man's allegiance and deterred him from thinking things out for himself.

They epitomized their crude ignorance of God and Nature by tying religion down to a set of dogmas, which placed the earth in a stationary position in the solar system and denied that any change ever takes place. They ran against the laws of gravity, the movement of the cosmic bodies, and the laws of evolution, all of which are now fully established and demonstrable. Claiming infallibility for their pronouncements, they were trapped by these contradictions, but lacked the grace or courage to admit their error. Indeed, how could they? After all, they pretended that everything they said was the word of God, not subject to change or contradiction.

3

It may be pointed out that some of the charges in this indictment, such as promoting wars and strife among nations and peoples, are more applicable to the Christian than the Jewish religion. That is true. Yet, when the Jews enjoyed on a small scale partial or complete autonomy, they also made their contribution to internecine strife and bloodshed. The strictures and outcries of the Prophets bear witness to that. The rabbis, too, built up a body of dogma and ritual that constricted the lives of their adherents and clogged their minds. The bogy of a "hereafter" was borrowed from others and used as a snare for reward or punishment in some vague, speculative, future existence.

Moreover, Christianity is an offshoot of Judaism. Had the early rabbis heeded the Prophets, at least those who had a social message, there might never have been a Christian religion. Between them they both "missed the boat." Instead of evolving a religion of truth and creating a world of justice, love, and understanding, they promoted superstition, dissension, internecine strife and hatred. It is not easy to determine whether more blood has been shed on account of religious wars or because of the secular and fiscal wars of kings and plutocrats.

The clergy succeeded in doing something more elusive and, in the long run, perhaps more inimical to progress. With skillful propaganda, religion insulated itself with such an impenetrable armor of moral halo, awe, and perfectionism that to challenge its citadel would require an Armageddon. While the citadels of militarism and plutocracy have at other times and places been successfully challenged and can still be challenged, that of organized religion, with chameleon agility, takes on new poses and coloration to make it appear it is on the side of the just and downtrodden. Theology managed to create a public opinion hostile to inquiry, skepticism, or criticism of either the Old or the New Testament. As time moves on, that attitude becomes more hostile and more menacing. The gains through Biblical criticism for a more enlightened and humane religion of a half century ago seem lost. We have actually slid backward and retrogressed.

Theology loves to flaunt in the faces of dissenters a challenge to them to answer the riddle of creation—the mystery of life. Because this challenge still is unanswered, theology claims that religion is triumphant and has been vindicated. But how? The answer is the fable in the beginning of Genesis of the creation of the world, including life, in six days. Anyone with imagination could have thought up such a fable, or even a more ingenious one, and invited everyone to accept it on faith, although it is contrary to all human experience or common sense. Indeed, a large majority of people, including many eminent theologians, no longer accept the story of creation in Genesis in its literal sense. They offer many and diverse theories and interpretations to reconcile the Genesis version with the now accepted scientific theory of the process of evolution in the geological and biological development of the world. Yet, in the face of these generally acknowledged facts, clergymen have the unmitigated gall and nerve to taunt science with failing to solve the riddle they themselves never even attempted to answer, other than by a mythological fairy tale.

Even our great modern press is a party to this hoax. At times it goes beyond that, by deliberately falsifying the facts in favor of theology and even lampooning science. The following is a verbatim reproduction of an article in the Sunday Edition of the *New York Times,* July 25th, 1948:

WASHINGTON, July 24. A grandmother stumped the atomic scientists today with her questions on the mystery of life and the fleeting soul at death. They said, at a news conference of the Atomic Energy Commission, that they were coming closer to the solution of how life begins.

In fact, with their radioactive isotopes they have finally discarded the last vestige of the mechanistic theory of the human body. But the soul? They have not got around to investigating it scientifically.

Mrs. Elizabeth May Craig, correspondent for several New England papers, put some members of the commission and its scientists on the spot.

"I would like to know if you think you are getting at the secret of where life begins?" asked Mrs. Craig, who also likes to throw elemental questions at President Truman.

The officials all looked at Dr. James A. Jenson, Director of its Biological Division.

"I think the answer would be yes," Dr. Jenson began bravely, "for the reason that it is impossible to push back the barriers of the knowledge of biology without understanding more about life."

Much later in the conference Mrs. Craig asked: "If you are finding out what life is, what is it that departs at death?"

Chairman David E. Lilienthal and the others again looked at Dr. Jensen.

"It would sound very silly on my part to reply that when life departs, death begins," Dr. Jenson replied. "That is about the size of it."

"You don't know what it is that happens?"

"There are a number of things that happen, of course," Dr. Jenson answered, "but what the precise thing is, the spiritual aspect of it, has not been investigated scientifically."

In the commission's report today, however, was new data rejecting the ancient belief that the body was like a combustion engine—the mechanistic theory that the body was a relatively inert structural system.

Isotopes produced at Oak Ridge, said the report, "show that all components of the body—the muscles, bones and teeth as well as blood, secretions and food stores—are in a constant state of breaking down and renewal."

"The multitude of life compounds involved in this process go through continuous and rapid chemical reactions, many of them reversible," the report continued. "Those not serving at any given moment as part of the fixed structure, and not excreted from the body, are combined into a metabolic 'pool' of life ingredients, available for use anywhere in the body."

Isotopes showed the dynamic life process was incredibly rapid. Salt, 'tagged' or irradiated, was injected in the arm and within a minute was observed passing through walls of veins, and coming out on the other side of the body in the sweat.

Now see how and where the actual facts given bear out the headline in large type, or the innuendo in the first paragraph or the general tenor of the entire article. If anything, it proves how far science progressed in solving the mystery of life.

CHAPTER IX

AN OPPORTUNITY FOR SERVICE

Finally, there is a golden opportunity for the rabbinate in the United States in a new field of green pastures. In the ghetto in East Europe, and in West Europe as well, the duties of the "rov" (ecclesiastical head) were many and arduous. He was the judge of all religious matters, and frequently the judge and arbitrator in civil disputes between private parties. He presided at religious rites, such as weddings, births, funerals and similar occasions, was consultant to members of the congregation on domestic problems, granted divorces, and in many communities acted as liaison between the Jewish community and the government. In addition, along with other members of the community, he had jurisdiction in matters of taxation and conscription, with official status and legal responsibility. In brief, he was the factotum of the entire Jewish community in its religious and civic life.

Under our democratic form of government, with its strict separation of church and state, the functions of the rabbi are necessarily limited and circumscribed. He is the religious head of the congregation, presides at weddings, and so forth, and is active in civic and social movements. But his services to the community are less essential than those of the rov or the rabbiner in the Jewish communities of Europe. Hence, his relation to his congregation is more tenuous and perfunctory.

This is a social loss and is to be regretted. At no time were Jews served by as fine a body of men as make up the present rabbinate. They are men of fine training and high culture and principles, and many of them are highly qualified for great leadership. That so much talent should be wasted or limited to an anaemic sermon once a week and on holidays and similar innocuous functions, is a great social loss. I use the words "anaemic" and "innocuous" without malice or intended sarcasm. Most congregations will not tolerate vigorous criticism of themselves or on issues that are considered "hot" or controversial or unpopular. If the rabbi becomes over-enthusiastic and is carried away by a crusading zeal, he will speedily be reminded that his domain is celestial, and that he is not to interfere in terrestial and practical issues.

At the same time, nearly all of the members of the congregation are concerned with private problems that plague them without end. Such problems may be domestic, arising from family conflicts, or they may grow out of social maladjustments, business difficulties, or many other causes which require objective appraisal. Who, by training and mental equipment, would be better qualified to advise and assist than one's spiritual mentor? Does this smack too much of psychiatry? Suppose it does? Who can possibly give greater comfort in distress than someone who can hold a confidence implicitly, and who is, at the same time, qualified by education, training, and temperament to give counsel and guidance?

Even now, under present conditions, rabbis frequently have to listen to a great many woes. But this is considered "extracurricular," and the individual member seeking advice often feels like a pest or intruder in worrying his pastor with his problems. On the other hand, the rabbi may have to intervene in certain situations; at such time, he may be regarded as an interloper who mixes in affairs not of his concern. The training now received by rabbinical graduates is very broad. It includes a preparatory academic course followed by a special course in theology at the seminary. The latter course embraces much that is esoteric, of which he makes but rare use in his professional career. Would not a course in psychiatry be of considerably greater value than some of the out-of-date subjects that he puts in cold storage when he leaves the seminary? Recently, a minister of a small community wrote a best-seller book, and in it he related how successful he had been in giving psychiatric aid. Answering a critic who protested that the minister, lacking medical training, was not qualified to give such treatments, he wisely replied that there is a wide margin where one can safely help borderline cases without elaborate medical training. But here one is tempted to ask, in relation to the rabbi: Why could not enough time be found in his eight long years of training to equip him with sufficient medical knowledge to deal with psychological problems which may entail some physical factor in producing or complementing them? Moreover, there is nothing to prevent a rabbi from pursuing such studies and inquiries after graduation as will aid him in the treatment of specific problems. What could be more satisfactory to the spiritual head of your community than to feel that he is making a real contribution to its members? It is certainly of vastly greater importance than worrying about the welfare of the communicant in some vague and hazy "hereafter." At present the cost of treatment by a professional psychiatrist is prohibitive for the average family or individual. The phenomenal success of Rabbi Liebman's book *Peace of Mind* is due not merely to its inherent excellence, but a good deal to the public's interest in, and hunger for, the information given in the book. Practical religion would advance its progress and scope by offering not only spiritual comfort, but by helping people to disentangle themselves from mental complications.

CONCLUSION

At the start of this book, I attempted to give a succinct and brief formula of its thesis and scope. How well or inadequately I performed that task, I shall perhaps never know. In the very nature of things one can hardly be objective and detached on his own performance. Nay, even the contemporary judgment of readers and critics do not always stand the test of time.

It is an axiomatic fact that the standing of a writer in public life, and/or his established reputation as a writer, have much to do with the way his work is received. This writer lacks both of these advantages. Fortunately for his peace of mind, neither of these elements, prestige as a public figure or established reputation as a writer, were definitive essentials for writing this book. As much as a favorable reception of it by the public would be a vindication for writing it and afford him the greatest spiritual joy he ever knew, these were not the objectives sought in its undertaking. Here a word of explanation for this attitude is in order.

In 1947, the writer published a book under the title *Mono-Juris*, wherein he essayed to explore the social, economic, and political conditions under which we live; though the discussion was cursory, it did cover most aspects of living. As in this work, the views and reflections which were entirely the author's were definitive, unequivocal, and as clear as he could express them.

But they dealt with matters and interests affecting every member of the community, irrespective of race or religion. For better or worse, Jews not only share in the problems and woes that confront the general citizenry, but have unique and additional problems thrust on them. This book addresses itself exclusively to these problems. A basic and recognized requirement for the solu-

[131]

tion of any problem is a thorough understanding of all elements and forces that create the problem. When that is achieved the panacea or solution is often self-suggestive. But to arrive at such an understanding, the analysis must be free of bias and partisanship. It must be accomplished with a maximum of objectivity and detachment. In scientific explorations, in or out of the laboratory, this method is known as trial and error. He tries one method, and, if it does not produce satisfactory results, he tackles the problem at another angle, sometimes using other materials, and/or other instruments.

In dealing thus with corporeal and material substances, you may waste time, money, and effort but at least you do not add to or complicate your original problem, nor do you run the risk of creating a monstrosity worse than your original problem. This is not so with human relations. That is because the laws governing physical and material things are, at least for experimental purposes, fixed and static. In dealing with the human psyche and reactions, there are too many imponderables. Take this as an instance: one of the current problems that plague us grows out of prejudice and social antipathies. Examples: anti-Semitism, anti-Catholicism or xenophobia in the native American stock. Somebody suggests legislation against them, the exorcism of these maladies by passing laws and penalizing their practice. When you do try that remedy, as has been tried in some instances, you find that instead of getting rid of the disease, you aggravated it, for the very attempt to eradicate hatred stimulated greater hatreds. Thus, you find that you lost time and effort, and, in some instances, money, just as in a laboratory experiment failure. But your headache is worse, and the problem even harder to solve.

Or take the paradoxical human conundrum, poverty. From time immemorial, human societies were confronted with the puzzle of how to satisfy the basic requirements of mere existence between the rich and the poor, the haves and have-nots. It is an economic problem, the task of getting enough things to go around. All human faculties were harnessed to solve this difficulty. Finally, through ingenuity, energy and science, the problem was licked. A solution was found. Through migration, science, discovery, and inventions, the way was found to produce in greater abundance than the collective demand of the world's population. Did it solve the problem? Yes, the problem of production was met, but it also created a Frankenstein—a curse almost as bad as the original evil. How to equate plenty with human greed, selfishness, and wickedness became the new puzzle, to which there is still no solution. Instead of bringing joy, contentment, and happiness, this chance to supply all legitimate human wants that actual and potential wealth made possible through science, is now the cause of such a scramble for its control and administration on a national and international level, that it threatens the very existence of civilization.

But one may logically ask: Why not resort to the same human qualities—intellect, ingenuity, science, and other resources—to meet this new problem? Here we are met with another of those phenomena that defy solution—a tendency to fall into a state of atrophy, a form of involuntary retrogression, and mental sluggishness. Call it cynicism, frivolity, hedonism, or folly. It spells a condition wherein one cares for naught but physical pleasure. He plunges into activities and practices which, if pursued in moderation, are not in themselves dangerous: for instance, sports, playing, love-making and other diversions. But, carried to excess, they undermine and frequently destroy one. Even when their effects are not that tragic, the result to the body politic, the social entity, is devastating. Such a person does not exert himself to think seriously or concern himself with collective or public matters. He becomes content to leave them to professional politicians. The only thing that matters to him is to get more thrills and ways of stimulating the appetite for them.

An extension of these activities is social and financial rivalries. In juxtaposition to the group literally doped by comfort and luxury, there is another malodorous class who may properly be termed the seducers of humanity. They are the so-called tycoons, "big shots," who wield much power and influence either through politics, or industry and finance. They are the insatiable ambitious upstarts, determined to reach their goal toward power, irrespective of the means they use. They corrupt everything they touch and are usually identified only during an exposé or scandal. They may at such time be swept out of power and even be disgraced, but such is the texture of our social and political system that it breeds a new crop of this vermin, and the performance repeats itself. Lately, when these foes of society are attacked by the decent elements of the community who are alert enough and courageous enough to challenge them, they countercharge their attackers with radicalism or worse, terming them communists—anything to confuse the public. These are the cycles of venality and sensationalism in public life, cycles of corruption, abuse, and suppression that continue until the public patience is exhausted and conscience aroused. Unfortunately, when that comes about, public fury often reaches such a degree that it goes berserk and hits the innocent and the guilty. Many a stormy reform crusade ended in a flop, bringing public disgust and discouragement.

History discloses that blueprints of synthetic remedies were concocted in theological, spiritual, material, and economical forms, which the promoters claimed would cure all evils. People were importuned to join this or that church or religious cult, or to work for a new and different political, and/or economic system, such as democracy or Marxism. Then, all problems would be taken care of. But it now appears from the tragic world situation of today that something more is required than a workable scientific plan to run the world's affairs. It is equally as important that the people have sufficient perception and understanding to put such a plan into effect and operate it. A world divided by racial and religious dogmas and differences will not do it. Certainly, labels and shibboleths alone will not do it. It may sound like a heartbreaking and painful task to bring the masses to such a level of intelligence. But in the final analysis that is the only panacea. Unhappily, there is no short cut to the achievement of that end. In one form or another, the same problem faced the ancients that faces us today. Now, too, there is only one known remedy. It is to nag and to blister the public conscience, to stir up the moral impulse that beats in every breast, so that people will study, examine, and consider everything that deals with human needs and human welfare; to realize that the peace and happiness of one's neighbor is essential to one's own peace and happiness. In a symbolic fashion that is what the ancient Hebrew prophets did in their day. Since then, scores of other prophets in one guise or another have kept on doing this. This is the meaning of every human appeal for the betterment and amelioration of human suffering and the promotion of human happiness.

To this purpose the author dedicates this and his other book. While, as already pointed out, he is handicapped by anonymity, lack of prestige or public influence, he enjoys some advantages which in part, at least, may offset these handicaps. He writes with a free mind not beholden to anyone or any organization or cause.

He does not have to reckon with the consequences of what he writes in his public career, which is behind him. While he seeks no notoriety and does not like to offend anyone, or any group or institution, yet he feels it his duty to express his thoughts when they are in the interest of human welfare and the clarification of evils that plague civilization. There are scores of such evils that need to be brought to light. Others see them also but dare not risk exposing them. If the author fills this gap, at least in part, he will be amply repaid for the effort and labor that went into this book.